R0174227528

05/01

Cooking *with*

Heart
& Soul

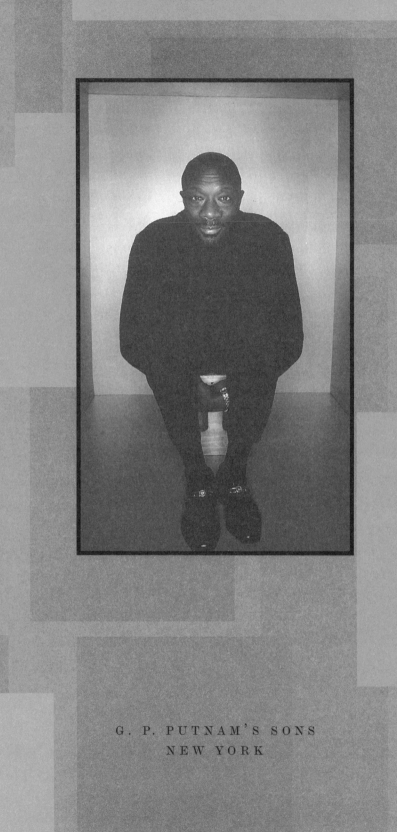

G. P. PUTNAM'S SONS
NEW YORK

Cooking *with*

Heart
& Soul

Heart & Soul Heart & Soul Heart & Soul Heart & Soul Heart & Soul Heart & Soul

Isaac Hayes

G. P. Putnam's Sons
Publishers Since 1838
a member of Penguin Putnam Inc.
375 Hudson Street
New York, NY 10014

Photographs that appear on pages 4, 56, 57, 72, 74 and 212 courtesy of Natalie J. DeVore

Library of Congress Cataloging-in-Publication Data
Hayes, Isaac.
Cooking with heart and soul / Isaac Hayes.
p.   cm.
ISBN 0-399-14656-3
1. Cookery, American.   I. Title.
TX715.H3936   2000   00-041746
641.5—dc21

Printed in the United States of America

1   3   5   7   9   10   8   6   4   2

This book is printed on acid-free paper. ∞

BOOK DESIGN BY AMANDA DEWEY

Acknowledgments

Wow, we finally got it done! It wouldn't have been possible without the blood, sweat, and madness of my team: Michelle Spence, Lourdes Melendez, Marie Mendes, Kissa Thompson, Natalie J. DeVore, Troy Taylor, and Jeffrey Morgan.

I owe a big debt of gratitude also to:

Pearlie Biles and Wendell Price, for their love and slammin' recipes.

My friends and business associates Christina "Kumi" Kumball, Diana George, Bruce Garfield, Cynthia Barnett, John Duff, Marilyn Ducksworth, and Susan DiSesa for believing in me and in this book.

Lu Woodard, B. Smith, and the celebrities who contributed their recipes, and the taste-testers, who put their waistlines at risk to make this the best book possible.

My road manager and good friend Benny Mabone, and my band members who have stuck with me through thick and thin.

My children, grandchildren, and family.

If I have forgotten anyone, it's only in words, not in my heart.

Thank you all for making this book a reality.

This book is dedicated to Rushia Addie Mae Wade, my grandmother and my heroine.

Your sacrifices for your family taught me about honor and responsibility. Your dignity in the direst circumstances taught me how to be proud of who and what I am. Your acceptance of others taught me about respect and ethics. Your tenacity taught me about patience and commitment. Your courage taught me about love.

Thank you, Mama. I will always love you. And you will always be in my heart, in my mind, and in my soul. You truly are my heroine. So rest, rest, noble lady, in the arms of God.

CONTENTS

Cooking *with* Heart & Soul

Growing Up in the Country

O n August 20, 1942, in a little tin-top house in a small town about thirty miles north of Memphis, Tennessee, I made my entrance into this world. I was delivered by a midwife, since it was rare to find a doctor in the country in those days. We lived with my grandparents Rushia, whom we called Mama, and Willie Wade, and my half sister, Willette, who is one year older than I am. My mother met and married my father after Willette's father died in a car accident. But I grew up not knowing either of them. My mother passed when I was only a year and a half old, and after she died, my father just left. (I didn't find him again until I was thirty years old.)

I learned later that my mother died in a mental institution, never really having recovered from my birth. I don't know many details, but I imagine the conditions in such institutions, especially for blacks in the South, were probably horrendous. I've got distant memories of someone who might have been her holding me, a feeling of the presence of someone, but I can't really remember her.

Our house in Covington was a simple but comfortable place. The walls and floors were made of wood, and the house was built up on bricks. I remember crawling under the house one day and playing with some matches I'd found. Lucky for all of us, my grandmother smelled the sulfur and caught me before I could burn the place down! We had to put newspaper in the chinks in the wall to keep the wind from coming through, but most of the time we were warm enough, with the potbellied stove fired up during the cold weather.

Like most of our neighbors, we didn't have electricity, so we had to rely on kerosene lamps and candles for light. We'd light the lamps on the mantel in the evenings and gather round to listen to the radio that ran off a huge Western Auto battery. We'd have to fiddle around with the antenna, which looked like a big fan on top, to get any decent reception. That radio was our link to the world outside Covington, and my first exposure to life beyond Tennessee.

One of my uncles was stationed overseas during World War II, and Granddaddy and my other uncles would listen for hours to news of the troops advancing across Europe. My uncle was wounded in Italy, shot in the leg. He survived by playing dead in a ditch until the medics rescued him. I still remember the day he returned from the war. We knew he was due to come home, but we didn't know when. We were working in the cotton fields when all of a sudden, far off in the distance, we saw this big cloud of dust. That's the thing about the country—you can tell a car is coming down the road even before you hear it because it kicks up so much dust. Someone shouted, "I see dust!" Everybody stopped and looked up, shading their eyes from the sun. "It looks like it's stopping at the house," one of my uncles announced. When a young man got out of the taxi, my grandfather shouted, "Ohhh, look at those shoulders, that's my boy, I know my boy!" Everybody stopped working and just ran to the house. That was a great day. For me, it was the day that the war ended.

The real heart of the house was Mama's kitchen.

With my father,
Isaac Hayes, Sr., Dallas, 1974.

We used to sit around her large kitchen table while she cooked. Sometimes she'd send me into the pantry to bring her dishes or utensils she had stored there. Great pots and pans hung from the ceiling near the stove, which was fueled by sticks of firewood.

Sometimes we'd get a delivery from a huge dump truck, a big load of firewood that would last us all winter. We'd keep it stacked outside, then go out and chop the wood as it was needed. Usually we burned coal in the living room and other parts of the house, though occasionally we'd have to burn wood for fuel.

But for the kitchen stove we used nothing but firewood. The stove in the kitchen was enormous, a big old "eight-eye" range with eight burners on top. It even had a reservoir attached to the stove to heat water. When I think of my grandmother, my most vivid memories are of her cooking at that stove.

I grew up eating what's now called southern soul food, but for us it was just the way Mama cooked every day. One of my favorite foods (and a recipe I've included here) was fried creamed corn with bits of bacon. If I close my eyes, I can smell the frying bacon and corn, which were served in a sauce of milk, butter, and flour, spiced with plenty of salt and pepper.

I learned how to cook from watching Mama work at that stove, although I never did any cooking myself when we lived in the country. That didn't stop me from butting in and making some trouble in the kitchen if I had the chance. One time I remember "helping" when my sister tried to season some peas. My family was off in the fields one morning, working hard and looking forward to coming home for a hot lunch. My grandmother told us, "Now, don't let my pot boil over." Willette said, "Okay," and she would have been fine except for my assistance.

After my grandparents left, I stepped up on a lard can and looked into the pot. I said to Willette, "You might want to put some salt in now." I was always prompting her to do all kinds of crazy stuff, and I guess what was crazier still is that she listened to me. Of course she put way too much salt in the pot. Before too long, everybody came home for lunch. They were tired and hot and hungry. We all sat down and said grace, then started to eat. As everyone dipped spoons into the peas and took a bite, they all froze. "Oh, it's salty, it's too salty!" they cried out. My grandmother asked us what happened, and I said quickly, "Willette did it, she did it!" We both got our hides tanned pretty good for ruining their lunch, and I don't think we ever did anything like that again.

Near the stove was our icebox—there was no such thing as a refrigerator in a home without electricity. The iceman would come once a day and deliver however many pounds you requested—ten, twenty, even fifty pounds if you needed it. The ice kept what was in the box cold for pretty much the whole day, and before everything warmed up, the iceman would be there again with a fresh load of ice. It's amazing to me to remember how well we managed without all the modern appliances we rely on today.

My grandmother kept the house spotless. She was always sweeping the floor, and her special secret was sprinkling water over the wood first because it helped collect the dust better. She used P&G soap—soap so strong it would take the skin off you. My grandmother washed our clothes with it on an old-fashioned washboard, wringing the wet clothes out herself. And when it came time for spring cleaning, washing with soap wasn't enough. She boiled our bed quilts in Parson's lye.

Out in front of our house, Grandfather had built a porch, while out in back we had a smokehouse. We'd hang hams and sausages and other meats in there to cure. We even had a barn over on one side where we kept the cattle. After we yanked raw peanuts out of the garden, we used to spread them out to dry up on the barn roof. I can still remember how great the house smelled when we roasted those dried peanuts in the fireplace in wintertime.

Rushia Wade, my grandmother.

When I think back on it, we were incredibly self-sufficient. We raised our own chickens, turkeys, and hogs. My grandmother churned her own butter, and we'd swap eggs for whatever food a neighbor had that we didn't. People would be walking down the road and stop by the house. "Can we have a little of your greens?" they'd ask, and my grandmother always answered, "Go ahead, help yourself." Or a neighbor would stop by the house with a whole string of fish that he'd caught and give my grandmother a couple of good-sized ones—sometimes bream or crappy, other times catfish or buffalo fish—and that was dinner. For dessert, Mama baked apple or peach pie, or made a cobbler from a mess of blackberries. In the country, you didn't know you were poor because everyone lived the same way.

You maybe knew you were living a meager existence in some ways, but you never wanted for food.

My family was well known in the community because my grandparents had seven kids—five sons and two daughters (my aunt and my mother). All their children lived in the area and worked their own pieces of land, except for their youngest son, who lived with us. One uncle lived with his wife across the field from us. She was known for baking coconut cakes and especially popular with me for making fresh pineapple ice cream. I loved to eat that ice cream so much, I'd do anything to taste it first. The kids—my cousins and I—would fight over the dasher (the mechanism for churning the ice cream in the freezer).

"Let me lick it," one of them would say. Then I'd insist that it was my turn, and a lot of the time I'd win. My aunt was a wonderful cook, and that pineapple ice cream is one of my best summer memories.

When I was seven years old, we moved from our house in Covington to a dairy farm in the area. It was "across the road and back aways," as we described country addresses. My grandfather worked for the dairy farmer there. I remember he owned a lot of Holsteins, and it was Granddaddy who had to put the milkers on the cows. It was a good way for him to get out of the fields and work indoors, but we didn't stay at the dairy farm very long.

At the time, in the years after World War II ended, a lot of country folks were moving into cities or up north to make a better life for themselves. Some of my uncles had gone ahead to Memphis already, and Granddaddy decided we should do the same.

I still remember the day we moved. We loaded everything we owned onto the truck. It must have looked like the Beverly Hillbillies—rocking chairs turned upside down, pots and pans hanging off the sides. As we drove to the city of Memphis, which was only about thirty miles away, it felt as if we were leaving forever the only world we knew.

Nothing could have prepared us for living in the city. We all went into culture shock, in part because we knew so few people there. We had to learn to adjust to a whole new way of life. I had never realized that in cities you had to *buy* food. We were used to just raising it on our own property. In the country, we'd been self-sufficient and in charge of our lives, but in the city, for the first time I truly knew what it meant to be hungry.

Succulent
Starters and My
Best Breads

Heart & Soul Heart & Soul Heart & Soul Heart & Soul Heart & Soul Heart & Soul Heart & Soul

Sweet Elizabeth's Salmon Croquettes

This is a variation on the salmon patties I often ate as a child. Back when I was in the first grade, I had a crush on a girl named Elizabeth. We didn't have lunch boxes or buckets out in the country; we carried our food in an old molasses pail. Whenever she unwrapped the wax paper and saw that she had salmon patties sandwiched between two biscuits, she always shared them with me. So now I'm sharing them with you. I like to use a commercial deep-fryer for this recipe, but you can use a frying pan if you prefer. *Serves 8 to 10*

2 14¾-ounce cans salmon, with juice
¼ cup chopped red bell pepper
¼ cup chopped green bell pepper
¼ cup chopped yellow onion
⅛ teaspoon Old Bay seasoning
⅛ teaspoon Chinese five-spice powder
⅛ teaspoon dried tarragon
⅛ teaspoon ground Jamaica allspice

½ teaspoon dried basil
½ teaspoon dried cilantro
2 whole eggs, beaten
2 egg yolks, beaten
½ cup cornmeal
½ cup all-purpose flour
½ 15-ounce can Italian-style bread crumbs
¾ cup canola oil

Put both cans of salmon with the juice in a large bowl. Break the salmon up gently with a fork and remove all bones. Add the peppers, onion, spices, and herbs and mix well. Gently mix in the eggs. Mix with your hands, add cornmeal and flour until the mixture holds together.

Form the salmon mixture into patties and lightly sprinkle with cornmeal. Coat the patties with the bread crumbs.

Heat a large skillet over medium heat and add the canola oil. When the oil is hot but not smoking, fry the croquettes until browned and heated through, turning once. Remove the croquettes from the pan and drain on paper towels.

Serve with Southern-Style Baked Grits (see page 29).

■ CHEF'S NOTE: Old Bay seasoning is a commercial mixture of cayenne pepper, graduated garlic, paprika, and sea salt. If you can't find it in your local market, you can always make up your own by mixing even portions of the ingredients.

Oscar-Winning Seafood-and-Crab Cakes

Crab cakes are a renowned southern specialty, and you'll find dozens of different approaches to this favorite appetizer. By adding shrimp and scallops, you produce a dish with a truly original flavor. Some chefs use almost as much bread as they do fish in their crab cakes, but when I promise you seafood in every bite, I deliver!

Serves 2 to 4

2 tablespoons butter
2 white onions, chopped
1 clove elephant garlic, minced
2 fresh sprigs thyme, finely chopped
1 fresh sprig parsley, finely chopped
1 roasted red bell pepper, finely chopped
1 pound lump crabmeat, picked over
6 tiger shrimp, peeled, deveined, and
　　chopped

2 large sea scallops, chopped
Pinch of sea salt
Pinch of cayenne pepper
1 egg yolk
⅓ cup plain dry bread crumbs plus
　　additional for coating
1 cup vegetable oil

In a medium skillet, melt butter over medium heat. Add onions, garlic, thyme, parsley, and bell pepper. Sauté for 4 minutes. Add crabmeat, shrimp, and scallops. Cook for about 3 minutes, until shrimp are pink. Stir in salt and cayenne pepper. Remove pan from heat and cool mixture for 30 minutes.

Add the egg yolk and bread crumbs to seafood mixture. Mix well with a fork.

Divide the mixture into four portions and shape each portion into a cake the size of your palm. Refrigerate for at least 30 minutes.

In a medium skillet, heat oil over medium-high heat. Sprinkle bread crumbs over the cakes; turn and sprinkle on other side.

Fry the cakes until golden brown and heated through, about 1 minute on each side, reducing the heat if cakes brown too quickly.

My Grandfather

My grandfather was a big man. He was tall (of course, everyone looked tall to me when I was a kid!), but it was more than height—he had a big presence. He was a leader in the community, someone to look up to in so many ways. Because I had no father to raise me, it was my grandfather who showed me how to be a man. He taught me, in words and in everything he did, to stand on my own two feet and be strong.

He had a terrific sense of humor, but far more important than making me laugh, he taught me how to behave. He'd say, "Be respectable, and never say something that you will regret." Or he'd say, "Don't ever lie. You should always be able to back up everything you say."

My sister and I loved helping him shave. He shaved with a straight razor, which he used to sharpen on a leather strap. We often fought over who got to put lather on his face from the shaving mug. Then we'd watch him as he carefully scraped away the lather until his face was as smooth as smooth could be.

I learned a lot of good things from my grandfather, but singing wasn't one of them. One of my favorite memories of my grandfather was when he'd come back from hunting with maybe five or six rabbits tied around his waist. We'd hear him singing long before we saw him emerge from a clearing in the woods. He had a horrible voice, but that never stopped him from singing at the top of his lungs. In church he would sing loud and wrong, and my grandmother would always hush him.

Carl Lewis's Jerked Catfish Woven on Cinnamon Kabobs

Most people know that Carl Lewis won a pile of gold medals at the Olympics, and some probably remember that he has a fine singing voice, too. But when you sample this original way of serving hot and spicy catfish, you'll quickly see that the man has a talent for food. Serve these hot!

Serves 4

4 2-inch-wide catfish fillets
4 4-inch cinnamon sticks
¼ cup Scotch Bonnet pepper sauce
1 tablespoon brown sugar
1 tablespoon sesame oil

¼ teaspoon cinnamon
¼ teaspoon grated nutmeg
¼ teaspoon ground ginger
½ onion, thinly sliced
½ red bell pepper, thinly sliced

Preheat oven to 350 degrees. Generously butter a small baking sheet. Poke a small hole 1 inch from the end of each catfish fillet and one in the middle of each. For each kabob, thread a cinnamon stick through the holes in one fillet so that the fillet forms an S on the cinnamon stick.

In a large, shallow glass bowl, combine the pepper sauce, brown sugar, oil, cinnamon, nutmeg, and ginger and mix well. Add the kabobs and rub with the spice mixture to make sure they are well seasoned. (Be sure to wear gloves during this process or the pepper sauce will irritate the skin.)

Place kabobs on the prepared pan and bake for 15 minutes. Garnish with the onion and bell pepper.

Pearlie's Soulful Cornbread Casserole

My friend Pearlie knows how much I love cornbread, so I like to think this recipe was created with me in mind. She says, "You can serve it as an entrée with a salad, plus some pinto beans or collard greens. Or you can use it as an hors d'oeuvre, cut into small, bite-size pieces."

Serves 8 to 10

1 pound ground beef or turkey
1 cup self-rising cornmeal plus additional for
    dusting pan
2 eggs
1 8½-ounce can cream-style corn

1 cup milk
½ cup vegetable oil
1 medium onion, chopped
3 jalapeño peppers, finely chopped
8 ounces extra-sharp cheddar cheese, grated

Preheat oven to 375 degrees. Grease a 13x9-inch baking pan and sprinkle with cornmeal. Place the pan in the oven until cornmeal browns, 5 to 10 minutes. Set pan aside.

In a large skillet over medium-high heat, brown meat, breaking it up with a spoon until crumbled as it cooks. Drain off the fat from the meat.

In a large bowl, combine the cornmeal, eggs, corn, milk, and oil. Spread half the corn-bread batter over the bottom of the prepared pan and sprinkle evenly with the meat. Layer onions, peppers, and cheese on top. Cover with the remaining batter.

Bake the casserole until top is golden brown, about 45 minutes. Let cool before cutting.

Alfre Woodard's Seafood Gumbo

Y ou know Alfre Woodard from such films as *Passion Fish* and *Down in the Delta,* which were filmed in the South and along the Gulf, where seafood is at its freshest. This recipe for gumbo combines so many flavors—shellfish, smoked poultry, and the vegetable at the heart of most gumbos: okra. You can make this with fresh okra if you can get it, but frozen okra is just as healthy and good-tasting in it. I like it best served over rice.   *Serves 6 to 8*

6 quarts spring water
6 skinless, boneless chicken breast halves, cut
*   into 2-inch pieces*
1 smoked turkey leg
¼ cup olive oil
4 onions, diced
5 green bell peppers, diced
2 cloves garlic, minced
2 teaspoons dried thyme leaves, crumbled
1 link smoked turkey sausage, cut into
*   ½-inch pieces*

1 16-ounce bag frozen cut okra
1 tablespoon fresh lemon juice
2 pounds shrimp, peeled and deveined
3 blue crabs
⅓ pound lump crabmeat
2 bay leaves
1 tablespoon Creole seasoning
Cayenne pepper to taste

In an 8-quart pot, heat water to boiling. Add the chicken and turkey leg and reduce heat to simmer.

In a large skillet, heat the oil over medium heat until hot but not smoking and sauté the onions until browned, about 15 minutes. Add the green peppers, garlic and thyme. Cook, stirring occasionally, until the vegetables have softened, about 10 minutes, and add to the chicken mixture.

Wipe out the skillet with a paper towel and heat the pan over medium heat. Add the sausage and sauté until browned. Add the okra and cook until thawed, about 5 minutes. Add the lemon juice (to remove slime from okra) and mix well.

Transfer the sausage mixture to the pot with the chicken and simmer, uncovered, over medium heat until chicken starts to break up into shreds and the gumbo is thickened, about 1½ hours.

Add the shrimp, crabs, crabmeat, and bay leaves to the gumbo and cover. Cook for 10 minutes.

Add Creole seasoning and cayenne and mix well.

Sharecropping

My grandparents and their neighbors were sharecroppers. A sharecropper works someone else's land and "shares" in whatever the cotton or other crop earns for the land's owner. The man who owned our property planted cotton. When we went to the local store to buy goods, the cost of what we bought would be charged against the cotton account. The system was designed so that a sharecropper just about never got out of debt or was able to go into business for himself. I guess this was a practice that started around the time that slavery ended, and the plantation owners needed a way to keep the workers farming their land.

Trouble was, sharecroppers never got ahead. All our hard work was just to keep our little piece of land and buy food. We might have a little change left over to buy some clothes, but they were usually overalls or other working clothes. We seldom had the money to buy something nicer, something that we would be proud to wear to church. My grandmother even made dresses for herself and Willette out of cotton flour sacks because they were made of printed cloth.

Still, when we lived in the country, I didn't know that we were poor. We had food on the table and clothes on our backs, and that seemed enough, at least for a seven year old who'd known little of life beyond Covington. But that was soon to change. . . .

Southern Quick Biscuits

I could have collected a baker's dozen of biscuit recipes, since each country cook has a slightly different version. But most agree that the less you handle the dough, the flakier the biscuits. Work quickly and confidently, make sure your oven is the right temperature (an oven thermometer is a good investment, since many oven dials aren't accurate), and be ready to serve your biscuits as soon as you can. *Makes 12 to 14 biscuits*

2 cups sifted self-rising flour
¼ cup vegetable shortening
⅔ cup buttermilk

Preheat oven to 450 degrees. Butter a large baking sheet.

In a medium bowl, combine the flour and shortening. With large fork or pastry blender, cut in the shortening until mixture resembles coarse meal.

Add buttermilk, stirring vigorously, to make a soft dough. Lightly roll or pat the dough on a floured board to about a ¾-inch thickness.

Cut out biscuits with a floured 2-inch round biscuit cutter and place on the prepared baking pan. Bake immediately for 12 to 15 minutes.

Quick Cornbread

The people who know me best know that I could eat cornbread every single day (and from time to time, I do!). I keep boxes of my favorite cornbread mix on hand in case the urge strikes when the stores are closed. If you don't have any buttermilk in the house, you can try making your own—just add a tablespoon of vinegar or lemon juice to a cup of regular or soy milk and let it sit for a few minutes. You can also try a cup of plain yogurt, though your batter won't be as wet.

2 cups self-rising cornmeal   *1 cup buttermilk*
1 cup Jiffy cornbread mix   *⅓ cup vegetable oil*
2 eggs

Preheat oven to 350 degrees. Grease a 13x9-inch baking pan with Pam nonstick cooking spray and heat in the oven while making the batter.

In a medium bowl, combine cornmeal and Jiffy mix. Add eggs, buttermilk, and oil, and mix until dry ingredients are thoroughly moistened, adding a little water if necessary.

Spread the batter in the prepared pan and bake until golden brown, 15 to 20 minutes.

North Memphis Hoecakes

Hoecakes are another cooking tradition that reaches back to slavery days, when these cornmeal cakes often served as breakfast for the field workers. They were traditionally fried in a skillet, then spread with molasses. Nowadays, this is another good way to get the flavor of cornbread in an easy accompaniment.

Serves 4 to 6

2 cups plain cornmeal
1 cup Jiffy cornbread mix
1 egg

Water
¼ cup canola oil or vegetable oil

In a medium bowl, combine the cornmeal, Jiffy mix, and egg and stir in enough water to make a thin, smooth batter.

In a large heavy skillet, heat enough oil to cover the bottom and, using a measuring cup, drop about ⅓ cup batter into the hot oil for each hoecake. Cook cakes until golden brown. Flip over and brown on opposite side.

Drain the hoecakes on paper towels.

Isaac's Breakfast of Champions

Over the years I've experimented to find what works best for me as a morning meal, especially when I've got a busy day ahead (which is most of the time). This is what I call "my breakfast of champions," my first choice for high-energy and easy digestion. I've listed the fruits I like to eat, but you can substitute any you prefer. The key to cooking brown rice is just to let the water boil out, but not too long. If you cook it too much, brown rice gets sticky.

Serves 2 to 4

1 cup brown rice, cooked according to
    package directions, with ¼ cup raisins
    added while cooking
3 tablespoons butter
¼ teaspoon cinnamon
¼ teaspoon grated nutmeg
½ cup sliced fresh peaches
½ cup sliced banana

½ cup sliced strawberries
½ cup sliced apples
½ cup blueberries
½ cup pineapple chunks
½ cup chopped walnuts
¼ cup maple syrup
1 to 2 tablespoons peanut butter per serving

In a large bowl, combine the cooked rice, butter, cinnamon, and nutmeg and mix well. Add the fruits, walnuts, and maple syrup and fold gently to mix.

What I do is put the peanut butter on the lip of the bowl, and when I scoop up some rice on my fork, I pick up a little of the peanut butter with it.

MEMPHIS MEMORIES

y family moved from Covington, Tennessee, to Memphis when I was seven years old, in hopes of finding a better life. But it didn't take long for me to understand that everything about our new home was different.

I couldn't get used to the noise and the people. All the streets in the city were paved, with the sidewalks concrete. I'd never seen a place like this, where people lived in houses so close together, and all the houses looked so much alike. In Covington, the houses were scattered this way and that, separated by fields of cotton or other crops. I'd grown up walking down the sides of dirt roads, ready to jump into the gully if a truck or car edged too close to where I was.

Of course, there were happy surprises about city living as well. The first time I saw a Popsicle man, I cried out, "Mama, you mean an ice cream truck comes by my house every day? Can I please have a nickel?"

And we now had electricity for the first time! I remember how excited I was, seeing my first television set at one of our neighbors' houses. Everybody crowded into their house, with a few even standing outside peering through the windows, watching that little black-and-white TV with the round screen. If you opened the door and sunlight poured in, you couldn't see the picture. "Close the door, the TV is on!" everyone would shout, and the door would slam shut.

In Memphis, the economy was said to be booming. It was the 1950s and times were supposedly prosperous, but you wouldn't know it by me. My grandfather found work in a tomato factory, where my uncle had a job, but the pay was low and the work exhausting. My grandmother stayed home and took care of us, at least until my grandfather became ill later on.

The first house we lived in was at 1244 Weakley Circle, but over the years we lived in many different places. Whether it was a one-room house, or a couple of rooms in the rear of a furniture store, we all had a hard time getting used to living in such cramped quarters—and with no land to grow food on, not even a backyard garden. So we had to buy whatever we could afford at the market. In these years, we were eating a very meager diet that was heavy on beans, potatoes, and rice. At that time, a loaf of bread cost a nickel; so did a bottle of Coca-Cola. (I remember when it became a dime and was totally beyond my reach.) Sometimes we'd make supper from a neck bone or pig's tail, and sometimes we had a jar of pig's feet and some chitterlings. No two ways about it—we were living low on the hog.

Memphis.

City living definitely took some getting used to. In the country, I'd used an outhouse as soon as I learned how, but in Memphis, our bathroom was indoors, and our toilet was the flush kind. At first, I found it scary sitting on the toilet, wondering if something was going to reach up and get me! I finally realized that nothing in the commode was going to bite.

In the country, we had to carry water into the house,

heat it on the stove, and pour it into a big washtub. So sitting in our Memphis bathtub, with water running out of the faucets, I used to feel like a millionaire. How could I be living in the jaws of poverty when I had all this hot water, just for the asking? But before long I began to realize how poor we really were.

After my grandfather got sick and had to stop working in the factory, times got really bad, and my grandparents had to go live with one of my uncles. There was no room there for me and my sister, so Willette moved in with an aunt, and I was staying with one of my aunt's ex-boyfriends. But he had a real drinking problem, and one night he got arrested. I was locked out of his apartment and had nowhere to go. I started sleeping in parked cars in a garage nearby, and later in an auto mechanic's shop. I felt like the odd man out, forced to live on my own before I was ready.

Finally, the family got back together and we moved into a small house. But by that time my grandfather was quite sick with a heart condition, and soon we moved to yet another part of town, where we lived in rooms over a church.

In November 1953, my grandfather passed. I was eleven years old and I will never forget the day. The morning he died, I remember seeing him lying in his bed before I left for school. His eyes were glazed, almost as if he were blind. His breathing was shallow and labored. I had never seen him this low.

My sister and I started walking to school, but halfway there I told her that I had a bad feeling and wanted to go home. So we turned around and headed back as quick as we could. When we got within earshot of the house, we heard my grandmother wailing and crying. She said my grandfather was dead. I ran up to his room and called his name. When he heard me, his eyes opened and his mouth gaped open like he was yawning. Then he just stopped breathing.

I remembered hearing somewhere—some old wives' tale, maybe—that if you rub the eyes of a dead person, then he won't be afraid to face death. So I gently rubbed his eyes closed. At first, his face had been contorted as if he were in pain, but then it just relaxed.

Looking down at his face brought back a flood of memories. I remembered when we were little that my sister and I would fight over who got to comb his hair. He was bald on top, but we would brush the fine little hairs around the side. And I thought of the time he'd cut my hair using manual clippers, insisting I stand still when all I wanted to do was go outside and play. "You stay here, son," he'd said firmly, "so I can cut your hair." It seemed to take him forever.

All those times, those experiences, came rushing back as I stood there next to his deathbed. His singing loud and wrong in church and Mama hushing him. And the evenings we'd spent together sitting on the front porch in Covington and singing Negro spirituals with the family. Even today, I'll hear one of his favorite songs, like "Eye on the Sparrow," and can't help but be moved by his memory. He's buried in Sommerville, near the church grounds where we used to go for the Hall's Picnic.

It was hard for me to see such a strong, powerful figure of a man melt away like that. After Daddy died, I had to become the man of the house. I couldn't play with the other kids anymore. I had new responsibilities, things I needed to do.

Now my grandmother, my sister, and I had to do whatever we could to make ends meet. For us, that meant doing migrant work whenever we could get it, mostly picking and chopping cotton.

We learned about a job by waiting on the Mississippi–Arkansas Bridge on the edge of town. A bus would pull up and the driver would say, "I'm going to so-and-so farm or this-and-such orchard." Someone would ask, "What are they paying?"

"Three dollars a hundred or ten dollars a day," he'd answer, meaning three dollars for picking a hundred pounds of peaches, or a dollar an hour for a ten-hour day chopping cotton. Once you understood the hours and the pay, when you knew the rules of the day, you'd jump on the bus and the driver would take you there.

I was going to school at the same time I was working. The Memphis Board of Education would allow kids whose families were living a very meager existence to take time off to pick cotton or other crops. Working in a peach orchard was better than going to school hungry and coming back home hungry. Sometimes I would make myself sick eating too many of those sweet, juicy peaches. I learned firsthand what a challenge it is for a child to learn and retain anything on an empty stomach.

Sometimes Mama took in laundry, or I would do odd jobs, if I could get them. I delivered groceries and ice in my child's wagon, sometimes getting a load of coal or firewood. I worked for a rag picker, and I cleaned bricks for construction crews. I even shined shoes on Beale Street. I loved watching and listening to the musicians who played down there, never dreaming that I would be coming back there as a musician myself.

I used to work sometimes for a mother and a daughter who lived across the street. I collected eggs in a henhouse to earn a nickel or a dime, and kids would tease me about it. Or maybe I'd earn a little bit by cutting someone's lawn. It might not have been much money, but it was honest work. And it paid off in other ways. If we were playing ball in our yard and the ball went onto the neighbor's property, I was the only one allowed to go get it because the neighbors knew and trusted me. Even as a youngster, I took a lot of pride in the work I did. It was my grandmother's example that instilled in me a strong work ethic. I was a real stickler for doing my best, no matter if the job was a humble one.

When I was in the seventh or eighth grade— I was about twelve or thirteen, I think—I started messing around in the

Beale Street, Memphis.

kitchen. The first thing I tried to make were biscuits, and I used my friends who were playing ball out in my yard as my guinea pigs. The first batch was hard as blocks of wood, because I added too much baking powder, but the kids ate them anyway. Kids will eat just about anything if you put a little jelly on it. They just kept eating those biscuits until I got them right. I wasn't giving up until my biscuits tasted as good as my grandmother's. Eating her food all these years made me want to learn how to cook—and to do it really well.

When I was sixteen, I first got paid for my cooking. I had been working as a busboy and dishwasher at a Memphis restaurant called Vanucci's, and from the day I was hired, I was eager to move up and become a cook.

Like so many restaurants in the South at that time, Vanucci's was segregated. So when I was promoted to short-order cook, I worked in the "Colored" section. I started with the basics—hot dogs and hamburgers, grilled-cheese sandwiches—and later did it all—fish, steaks, eggs and bacon for breakfast.

When I first started cooking, I'd peek out the pickup window and watch the folks eat my food. I'd be worrying, "Is it good? Oh, I hope they aren't going to come back and complain!" The truth is, I never got any complaints. It was a fun job and I stayed there about a year. Then I was back doing odd jobs again.

I took a job at a neighborhood grocery store as a delivery and stock boy. I also cleaned up the butcher block behind the meat counter at the end of the day. I got paid in groceries. It wasn't much of a job, but it kept my sister, my grandmother, and me eating. Eventually the owner and I parted ways, when he told me to do something I felt was wrong. He threatened to fire me if I didn't do what he told me to do. But even though I didn't know where our next meal was coming from, I walked out. It was the principle of the thing. I felt proud that I didn't give in.

Times like that stay with you, no matter where your life takes you later on. Back then, when the world would get me down, and I'd tell my grandmother that the kids were teasing me or that I was hungry or tired, she would say to me, "Just keep on living, son. Keep on living."

Southern Sides and Country Vegetables

Southern-Style Baked Grits

Grits are simply the comfort food of the South. We eat them for breakfast and dinner, with eggs in the morning and pork at night. They soak up all those meat juices and flavorful sauces. When they're good, they're great, and when they're just ordinary, they're still a taste of childhood we just don't outgrow. This is the version that I like best. (If your grocer doesn't stock bacon-flavored cheese, order it on-line from www.wisconsincheesemart or other suppliers.)

Serves 4 to 6

4 cups water	*6 ounces bacon-flavored cheese*
½ teaspoon salt	*½ cup milk*
1 cup grits	*2 eggs, beaten*
1 tablespoon butter	*Pinch of paprika*
1 clove garlic, minced	*½ cup grated cheddar cheese*

Preheat oven to 350 degrees. Butter a 2-quart baking dish.

In a medium saucepan, combine water and salt and heat to boiling. Stir in the grits and simmer over medium heat until tender, about 15 minutes.

Meanwhile, in a small saucepan over medium heat, melt the butter and sauté the garlic until fragrant, about 1 minute. Add the bacon-flavored cheese and heat, stirring, until melted. Add the milk and stir until blended.

Add the garlic mixture to the grits and stir in the eggs and paprika. Spread the grits mixture in the prepared baking dish and bake until set, about 40 minutes.

Remove the grits from the oven and sprinkle with grated cheese. Bake until cheese is melted, about 15 minutes longer.

Corn Pudding

This is the kind of corn pudding I loved when I was a child, creamy and full of corn flavor. The egg whites make it puff up just a little, so it looks good when you bring it to the table! It's especially good as a side dish with ham.

Serves 6 to 8

½ pound frozen corn kernels
1 15-ounce can cream-style corn
1½ cups milk
1 4-ounce jar chopped pimientos, drained
1 medium green bell pepper, chopped
3 tablespoons all-purpose flour

3 tablespoons butter, melted
2 teaspoons sugar
½ teaspoon salt
4 egg whites, beaten until stiff
3 slices cooked bacon, crumbled

Preheat oven to 350 degrees. Generously butter a 3-quart baking dish.

In a large bowl, combine the corn kernels, creamed corn, milk, pimientos, bell pepper, flour, butter, sugar, and salt and mix well. Fold in the egg whites and gently spread in the prepared dish.

Bake pudding until it is slightly firm, about 1 hour. Sprinkle with the bacon and serve.

"Hot Buttered" Fried Creamed Corn

Mama used to make this dish for me on her wood-burning stove in the kitchen. When I make it nowadays, it lets me travel back in time in an instant and relive those happy times. There is nothing like the smell or taste of fresh-cooked bacon mixed with fried corn.

Serves 4 to 6

6 ears corn
3 slices bacon
2 tablespoons butter
1 tablespoon all-purpose flour

1 cup evaporated milk, warmed
Salt to taste
Pepper to taste

Cut the kernels off the ears. Heat a large skillet over medium-high heat, add the bacon, and fry until crisp. Drain on paper towels and crumble.

In the drippings in the pan, sauté the corn kernels until lightly browned. Add the butter and heat until melted. Stir in the flour until smooth and gradually stir in the evaporated milk. Stir in the crumbled bacon and cover and cook until the sauce is thickened, about 10 minutes. Season with salt and pepper.

"Sock It to Me" Squash Casserole

Country food has the reputation of sticking to your ribs, and this hearty side dish deserves that description. Freshly grated sharp cheddar is my choice in this recipe, which emerges from the oven golden and good.

Serves 4 to 6

1 teaspoon vegetable oil
6 to 8 medium yellow squash, sliced into
    rounds
1 large white or yellow onion, thinly sliced
1 cup evaporated milk
12 ounces cheddar cheese, grated
1 4-ounce jar chopped pimientos, drained

2 egg whites, beaten until stiff
1 teaspoon salt
Dash of ground white pepper
1 cup bread crumbs or Pepperidge Farm
    Herb Stuffing Mix
¼ cup butter, melted

Preheat oven to 350 degrees. Grease a 2-quart baking dish with vegetable oil.

Place squash and onions in a steamer and cook until soft enough to mash, about 10 minutes. Place the mashed vegetables in a large bowl and add the evaporated milk, cheese, pimientos, egg whites, salt, and pepper. Fold mixture gently to combine. In a separate bowl, combine the bread crumbs and butter and mix well.

Spread half of the bread-crumb mixture over the bottom of the prepared baking dish. Top with the squash mixture and sprinkle with the remaining bread-crumb mixture.

Bake until golden brown, 30 to 40 minutes. Serve while hot.

Cheddar Baked Beans

Baked beans are truly an all-American dish, but it's the variations that cooks across the country have created that make ordering them on the road such an adventure! You never know exactly what you'll get—how sweet or tangy or thick and rich the sauce will be. To make life easier, I often use canned baked beans in this recipe. But if you have the inclination and just a little more time, you can start from scratch using dried beans; just follow the instructions on the package to get them ready to flavor and bake.   *Serves 4 to 6*

1 28-ounce can baked beans
½ cup chopped onion
½ cup chopped red bell pepper
½ cup chopped green bell pepper
1½ teaspoons minced fresh cilantro
¼ teaspoon Chinese five-spice powder
¼ teaspoon dried basil

⅛ teaspoon curry powder
⅛ teaspoon ground cardamom
Pinch of ground black pepper
¼ to ⅓ cup honey or maple syrup, according
   to taste
1 tablespoon butter
1 cup cubed sharp cheddar cheese

Preheat oven to 350 degrees.

Place the beans in a 1½-quart baking dish. Stir in the onion, peppers, seasonings, and honey or maple syrup. Dot with the butter and top with the cubes of cheddar cheese.

Bake for 30 minutes. When the cheese is melted and bubbly and you can smell the spices, it's ready!

Doug E. Doug's Homemade
Baked Beans with Love

Talented artist Doug E. Doug says that beans have always had a special place in his life. He adds, "In the immortal words of Clark Terry, passed from Bill Cosby to me, 'The bean doesn't have an enemy.'" You'll notice that the love isn't listed in the ingredients—you'll have to add that yourself!

Serves 2 to 4

1 cup spring water
½ cup tomato paste
3 cups cooked navy beans

2 teaspoons brown sugar or honey
2 teaspoons butter
½ teaspoon all-purpose flour

Preheat oven to 300 degrees.

In a small saucepan, mix the water with the tomato paste until smooth and cook over medium heat for 20 minutes.

In a 1½-quart baking dish, combine the beans, brown sugar or honey, butter, and flour. Stir in the tomato-paste mixture.

Bake for 15 to 20 minutes. These are great served with ribs.

Fourteen-Bean Explosion (Third State)

I like to use organic foods whenever I can get them, and that includes the different varieties of dried beans called for in this recipe. Check the packages to determine which ones need presoaking, or consult the store manager if you purchase your beans in bulk at a health food store. Most people resist using dried beans because they don't want to take the time to soak them overnight. But you'll be surprised to discover that many dried beans need little advance preparation.

Serves 8 to 10

1 cup dried garbanzo beans
1 cup dried black turtle beans
1 cup dried adzuki beans
1 cup dried navy beans
1 cup dried large lima beans
1 cup dried mung beans
1 cup dried hato mugi (Job's tears)
1 cup dried red beans
1 cup dried green beans
1 cup dried yellow lentils
1 cup dried great northern beans
1 cup dried black-eyed peas
1 cup dried pinto beans

1 cup dried soybeans
2 quarts spring water
2 tablespoons pickling spice with peppercorns (remove whole cloves)
2 bay leaves
1 fresh sprig oregano, chopped
1 teaspoon chili powder
Pinch of cayenne pepper
½ cup chopped onion
½ cup chopped red bell pepper
½ cup chopped green bell pepper
1 tablespoon maple syrup or to taste

In a large pot, cover the beans with water and soak overnight. Drain and rinse in several changes of water.

In a large pot, combine the soaked beans with the spring water and heat to boiling over high heat. Add the pickling spice, bay leaves, oregano, chili powder, and cayenne and reduce the heat to simmer, and cook until the beans are tender, 2 to 3 hours. Add the onions and peppers and cook for 10 minutes. Stir in the maple syrup.

Spicy Green Beans in Marinara Sauce

Remember the saying "Necessity is the mother of invention"? Well, sometimes, so is boredom. One night when I was feeling a little tired of the same old green beans, I opened a jar of my favorite sauce and cooked them in it. Suddenly I had a new way to make those same-old, same-old beans. (Feel free to use fresh beans in this recipe, but it's always good to keep a bag or two of frozen ones on hand.)   *Serves 2 to 4*

1 10-ounce package frozen green beans   *Pinch of cayenne pepper*
½ 14-ounce jar marinara sauce   *Salt to taste*
½ teaspoon chili powder   *Ground black pepper to taste*

In a medium saucepan, cook the green beans according to package directions. When the beans are almost done and most of the liquid has been reduced, add the marinara sauce, chili powder, cayenne pepper, salt, and pepper. Stir well. Cook until desired doneness.

Jersey City Lima Beans

This dish isn't exactly native to New Jersey, though the state does produce an awful lot of the nation's lima beans. But this is the way they like to serve them there—or at least that's the way I've heard it. This is one of those cases where frozen vegetables are your best choice.

Serves 4 to 6

1 20-ounce package frozen lima beans
1 28-ounce can crushed tomatoes
1½ cups chopped onions
2 large bell peppers, chopped
1 clove garlic, minced

8 ounces cheddar cheese, grated
1 teaspoon lemon pepper
1 teaspoon dried marjoram
Salt to taste
4 tablespoons butter, melted

In a large saucepan, cook the lima beans in water according to package directions, adding the tomatoes, onions, bell peppers, and garlic while cooking. Cook over low heat, stirring frequently, until vegetables are tender and liquid evaporates slowly, 20 to 30 minutes.

In a small bowl, combine the cheese, lemon pepper, marjoram, and salt. Mix well and stir into the lima bean mixture. Add the melted butter and mix well.

Pour into a serving bowl.

Growing Our Own

When we lived in the country, my grandmother kept a big kitchen garden, where she grew lots of vegetables. We grew cabbages and all kinds of greens—mustard and collard greens, turnip greens—plus rutabagas and peas, and okra, butter and snap beans, and beets. We pulled potatoes from the ground, both white and sweet, and plucked tomatoes from the vine. We raised beautiful fruit, too, figs and strawberries, melons and berries of all kinds.

We even had enough land to grow corn. We would take most of our corn to a gristmill to be ground into cornmeal for bread and baking. We could grow popcorn in the cotton field, because it would come up just about anywhere. When it was ripe, we'd take the ears of corn off the stalks and throw them in the loft of the barn to dry. In the wintertime, what a treat it was to pop the popcorn over a roaring fire!

Lucky Black-Eyed Peas

This is a good example of what I'd call southern smarts—making a little bit of meat stretch to feed the family by cooking it together with a potful of peas! I ate these so often when I was young, you might think I'd never want to see them on my plate again. But you'd be wrong—they're still one of my favorites. These are great for your New Year's Day feast.

Serves 2 to 4

1 cup dried black-eyed peas
1 smoked ham hock or smoked turkey leg
About 3 quarts spring water

1½ teaspoons sugar
Salt to taste
Ground black pepper to taste

In a large bowl, cover the black-eyed peas with water and soak overnight. Drain and rinse in several changes of water.

In a large pot, combine the ham hock or turkey leg with 2 quarts of the spring water and heat to boiling over high heat. Simmer until the meat is tender but not falling off the bone, about 20 minutes.

Add the peas, sugar, salt, pepper, and enough spring water to cover the peas. Heat to boiling, reduce the heat to low, and gently simmer the peas until tender, about 2 hours.

Pipin' Peas with Onions

For me, what makes a dish of vegetables extraordinary instead of just a plain old side dish is the seasoning. I've become a big fan of Spike, a premixed combination of herbs and spices that really awakens the taste of certain foods. I buy the salt-free kind, but if sodium isn't a concern for you, try them both. Another good choice is Mrs. Dash.   *Serves 2 to 4*

10 pearl onions, peeled
2 cups fresh green peas
1 teaspoon olive oil

Spike or Mrs. Dash salt-free seasoning
1½ teaspoons minced fresh basil, or
⅛ teaspoon dried

In a small saucepan, boil the onions until slightly tender, about 5 minutes. Add the peas and cook until the vegetables are tender, about 5 minutes. Drain.

In a medium skillet, heat the oil over medium heat. Add the onions and peas and cook, stirring constantly, until the onions brown. Add Spike seasoning and basil and stir well.

Remove from heat and serve with Isaac's Roasted Crispy Chick (see page 113).

"Mean Green" Collard Greens

We used to have a patch of greens growing wild not far from our house, so we never worried about not having enough to share with the neighbors. Later, when I was out on the road with the band, my backup singers would sometimes cook soul food for us on a couple of hot plates. No matter where we might be playing, we got a little taste of home— ham, skillet cornbread, rice, and beans, and one of my special favorites: seasoned collard greens.

Serves 2 to 4

3 cups water
8 ounces smoked turkey parts
1 pound collard greens, washed, trimmed of
    thick stems and veins, and cut crosswise
    into 2-inch-wide pieces
1 medium onion, finely chopped

¼ cup maple syrup
1 tablespoon vinegar
2 bay leaves
Pinch of cayenne pepper
Salt to taste

In a large pot, heat the water to boiling over high heat and add the turkey parts. Reduce heat to medium and cook until meat is tender but not falling apart, about 20 minutes.

Add the collards to the pot with the turkey and cook greens until tender, about 30 minutes. Add the onion, maple syrup, vinegar, bay leaves, cayenne, and salt and mix well. Return mixture to boiling. Drain.

Serve with pickled peaches or pickled beets.

Fried Kale with Turnip, Mustard, and Collard Greens

We always cooked with wild greens out in the country, but now I visit a local green market to "gather" my greens for frying. I like the way the four different greens complement one another in this recipe, so do try to use equal amounts of them when you cook them up.

Serves 6 to 8

1 bunch kale
1 bunch mustard greens
1 bunch turnip greens
1 bunch collard greens
⅓ cup olive oil
1 medium onion, chopped
1 clove garlic, minced

1 cup water
1 bay leaf
1 tablespoon vinegar
1 tablespoon maple syrup
Salt to taste
Pepper to taste

Wash all greens and trim off stems and thick veins. Cut leaves crosswise into 2-inch-wide pieces and mix together.

In a deep skillet, heat olive oil over medium-high heat. Cook onion and garlic until fragrant, about 1 minute. Add greens and cook, stirring occasionally, until softened, about 15 minutes, reducing heat as necessary to keep the greens from sticking to the pan.

Add the water, bay leaf, vinegar, maple syrup, salt, and pepper to the greens and cook until desired doneness, at least 1 hour, adding extra water if necessary.

Memphis Summer Fried Green Tomatoes

If you thought fried green tomatoes was just the name of a movie, you've got a real treat coming. This dish is the true taste of summer for this Memphis kid. I've always loved to eat my fried green tomatoes with fried catfish, so for the genuine experience, pair them on your menu!

Serves 4 to 6

3 firm green tomatoes
About 1½ cups vegetable oil
Salt to taste

Pepper to taste
1 cup plain cornmeal

Wash tomatoes and cut crosswise into slices about ⅓ inch thick. Pour enough of the oil into a large, heavy skillet to measure ⅛ inch deep and heat over medium heat until hot.

In batches, sprinkle the tomatoes with salt and pepper, dip into cornmeal, and fry on both sides until browned, adding more oil to pan as necessary. Drain tomatoes on paper towels.

Spicy Stewed Tomatoes

Home-stewed tomatoes may sound like a recipe for people with too much time on their hands, but these are so much better than any canned variety I've tried. If you'd like to try a variation on this dish, add a half cup of sun-dried tomatoes as the mixture begins to reduce.

Serves 2 to 4

4 ripe beefsteak tomatoes, sliced
1 tablespoon maple syrup
1 tablespoon apple cider vinegar
1 teaspoon chopped fresh basil
1 teaspoon chopped fresh sage

1 teaspoon chopped fresh oregano
Sea salt to taste
Pinch of cayenne pepper
1 tablespoon butter (optional)

In a medium saucepan, combine the tomatoes with the syrup, vinegar, herbs, salt, cayenne, and enough water to cover. Heat to boiling, reduce heat to low, and simmer until the tomatoes begin to fall apart, about 20 minutes.

Add the butter, if using, and stir gently. Cover and simmer about 5 minutes longer.

Smashing Mashed Potatoes

No matter whether you grew up in the South or somewhere else in the country, I'd be willing to bet that mashed potatoes are one of your comfort foods. Some people like to leave the skins on, but not at my house. I've suggested a range of how much evaporated milk and Miracle Whip to use—it depends on how creamy you like your mashed potatoes. I have one unbreakable rule in my house: No lumps.

Serves 4 to 6

2 pounds boiling potatoes, peeled
4 tablespoons butter
1½ cups Carnation evaporated milk

2 to 3 tablespoons Miracle Whip
Sea salt to taste

In a large saucepan, cover the potatoes with water. Cover, heat to boiling, and simmer the potatoes until they are fork-tender, about 30 minutes.

Drain the potatoes and mash with a potato masher until you remove all the lumps. Stir in the butter, evaporated milk, and Miracle Whip until thoroughly blended. Season with sea salt.

Serve these with Ike's "Three Tough Guys" Turkey Meat Loaf (see page 133).

Sweet, Sweet Potatoes

When I was younger, I used to make this recipe with white or brown sugar. Now I prefer the taste of maple syrup.

Serves 2 to 4

2 cups peeled, sliced sweet potatoes
⅓ cup maple syrup
¼ cup water

2 tablespoons butter
¼ teaspoon cinnamon
¼ teaspoon grated nutmeg

In a large saucepan, combine the potatoes, syrup, water, butter, cinnamon, and nutmeg and heat to boiling. Cover and simmer until the potatoes are tender and the liquid turns syrupy, about 20 minutes.

If all the water boils off before the potatoes are done, add more water.

Serve hot.

"Hot and Steamy" Asparagus

Spike, a commercial blend of herbs and spices, is widely available in most parts of the country. If you can't locate it where you are, some other spices to try include tarragon or chervil. Another variation: Sprinkle a bit of curry powder into the melted butter before you brush the spears.

Serves 2 to 4

1 bunch asparagus, tough ends trimmed
3 tablespoons butter, melted

Spike seasoning to taste
Sea salt to taste

Place the asparagus in a steamer basket. Brush the spears with the melted butter and sprinkle with Spike and sea salt.

Cover and steam for 5 to 10 minutes or until as tender as desired, depending on taste and thickness of asparagus.

Sautéed Spinach

Pearlie cooked this for me when I was advised to eat spinach because of a suspected ulcer. Well, it turned out I didn't actually have an ulcer, but by then I'd come to love this way of serving spinach.

Serves 4 to 6

1 tablespoon olive oil
2 cloves garlic, chopped
1 2-pound bag fresh spinach, washed well,
    tough stems removed

Sea salt to taste
Ground black pepper to taste

In a large skillet, heat oil over medium heat and sauté garlic until it just begins to brown. Add the spinach and sauté until wilted and heated through.

Sprinkle spinach with sea salt and pepper.

Serve with Salmon Baked in Foil for a quickie meal (see page 85).

Pearlie

I first met Pearlie Biles in 1969 through her sister, Earlie, who worked for Stax Records, where I was a writer/producer. One evening when I dropped Earlie at her apartment, Pearlie was about to make dinner and asked me to join them. But I had to ask Pearlie for some special dishes because I thought I was getting an ulcer. She gave me creamed spinach and the most wonderful mashed potatoes. I went back often and always contributed to the cost of the meals she made for us. Pearlie still remembers her reaction when I handed her a one-hundred-dollar bill to buy groceries: "I was thoroughly impressed. As a twenty-something girl, I had not held many one-hundred-dollar bills in my hands. That was a huge amount of money in 1969. You can believe that I gave *that* meal my very best."

Pearlie, who was working for a company that promoted health and nutrition products, sparked my interest in the power of vitamins to help ensure good health and promote physical fitness. One evening I went with her to a sales meeting and was so impressed with the presentation that I started taking the vitamins—and I've been on a vitamin regimen ever since.

Pearlie Biles at the Academy Awards, 1972.

But I really got to know Pearlie well when she got a job in the accounting department at Stax, and not long thereafter she became my personal bookkeeper. Over the years we've talked of going into the food business together—perhaps opening a restaurant or café. I even persuaded her to take cooking classes, with an eye toward the future.

In 1992, Pearlie decided to go back to college and pursue a degree in hospitality management, and I'm happy to report that we're working together again on my food business— and she still cooks for me whenever we're in the same town!

Candied "Ooooh Baby" Carrots

I'm not sure who first got the idea to sweeten up an already sweet vegetable like carrots, but this tasty side dish fills your kitchen with a great aroma. Kids who usually shove their vegetables to the side of the plate are sure to enjoy these.

Serves 2 to 4

2 cups baby carrots, rinsed
⅓ cup maple syrup
2 tablespoons butter

2 tablespoons water
¼ teaspoon cinnamon
¼ teaspoon grated nutmeg

In a large saucepan, cover the carrots with water. Cover pan and heat to boiling. Simmer the carrots until fork-tender, about 10 minutes. Drain.

Combine the carrots, maple syrup, butter, water, cinnamon, and nutmeg in the same pan and cook over medium heat, stirring, until the liquid is syrupy and the carrots are well coated.

Garden-Fresh Grilled Vegetables

I've listed a dream vegetable garden's worth of veggies to be grilled in this manner, but I don't expect you to combine all of them at one time! The more, the merrier, of course, so line up as many different colors, textures, and tastes as you can. I usually make these using metal skewers, but if you want to use bamboo sticks, make sure you wet them first so they don't get burned.

Onions, cut into 1-inch cubes or cut into wedges through the root
Peppers, cut into 1-inch cubes or wedges
Carrots, cut into 1-inch pieces
Zucchini, cut into 1-inch rounds or chunks
Squash, cut into 1-inch rounds or chunks
Corn on the cob, cut crosswise into 1-inch pieces
Broccoli, cut into florets large enough to skewer
Eggplant, cut into 1-inch rounds or chunks

Cabbage, cut into wedges
Sweet potatoes, cut crosswise into ½-inch pieces
Mushrooms, whole or halved, if large
Red potatoes, cut in half
Tomatoes, quartered into wedges, or use whole cherry tomatoes
Olive oil
Salt
Pepper

Wash and skewer vegetables. Brush with olive oil and sprinkle with salt and pepper. I place a sheet of aluminum foil on the grill after getting the grill mark on my vegetables so they can cook without direct heat, especially when I cook potatoes.

Steamed Vegetables

This is my good old reliable way of preparing vegetables anytime at all. I've suggested the vegetables that I prefer, but feel free to choose your own. I always try to buy organic whenever I can. I sometimes eat this for lunch or dinner, on its own or as a complement to the Roasted Crispy Chick (page 113) or Salmon Baked in Foil (page 85).   *Serves 6 to 8*

1 cup broccoli florets
1 cup cauliflower florets
1 cup chopped fresh spinach
½ cup fresh peas
½ cup corn kernels
2 carrots, scraped and cut into strips

½ Vidalia onion, sliced
1 tablespoon butter
Spike seasoning to taste
1 tablespoon fresh sage, or 1 teaspoon dried
1 tablespoon soy sauce

Place vegetables in a steamer basket over pot of simmering water or on a rack over boiling water in a large saucepan. Cover and steam vegetables until just cooked, crisp-tender, about 10 minutes. Transfer vegetables to a large serving bowl.

Melt the butter in a saucepan and stir in the Spike, sage, and soy sauce. Pour the butter mixture over the vegetables and toss to coat.

EDUCATING ISAAC

y first teacher was really my grandmother. She was the one who instilled in me my love of books and learning. She read to me all the time when I was a boy: *The Arabian Nights,* stories about the noble knight Roland, and tales of King Charlemagne. Books gave me the chance I wanted to explore the world beyond Tennessee.

It was from books that I learned about the different countries of the world, and from books that I discovered how other kids lived. I got to experience cultures from every part of the globe through the books I read, with Mama and on my own. I was always interested in the lives of children in faraway places—the little Dutch boy with his wooden shoes, the child in Argentina who lived on the great pampas. I recall reading about the gauchos who rode the South American plains, hunting with a bolo that would wrap around an animal's legs and stop it in midgallop.

By the light of a kerosene lamp, Mama read to me from the Bible, too, bringing all those stories to life. All these years later, I still remember how much I loved hearing her read.

Where we lived in Covington, the schoolyard was just across the street from our house, so I started going to school when I was just three years old. As soon as I could, I'd run across the road and into the schoolhouse when the bell rang. I wasn't officially enrolled, but as long as there was an empty seat, I sat with the older kids in that one-room schoolhouse and took it all in. By the time I turned six years old, when I should have been in the first grade, I already had a third-grade education. There were twenty-five or thirty kids in the school at that point. Miss Johnson taught grades one through three. Miss Ora was the principal of the school and also taught the higher grades.

Throughout my life, even when I wasn't aware of it, teachers have looked out for me. They paid attention when I showed them I wanted to learn. And later, when I dropped out of high school for a while, it was my teachers who refused to let me give up on myself.

I dropped out of high school for the same reason I think a lot of kids still do today. I was embarrassed about the way we lived, particularly when we had little or no food. And I was ashamed of the way I looked—my clothes and my shoes were old and tattered.

Back in Covington, I didn't feel poor, because everyone around me was living the same way. Everybody wore raggedy clothes in the country, but at least we never wanted for food. When we moved to Memphis, I realized how poor we were—and I hated how it made me feel. The struggle to survive finally got to me, I think. I looked down at my shoes one morning, and they were so worn out, they had holes in them and the soles were flopping around. I felt too ashamed to go to school, although I really did love it there. So that day I went in one door of the school, walked out the other side of the building, and decided not to go back.

(I'd reached the age where you start noticing girls and they start noticing you. Some of the guys even had cars, and they could pick up their girlfriends to go out. But my family had no car for me to borrow, and I hated walking around in

With the legendary bluesman B. B. King at my alma mater, Manassas High School in Memphis, when I received my marker, 1997. PHOTOGRAPH © ERNEST C. WITHERS PHOTOGRAPHER.

raggedy clothes. I even picked a fight with my girlfriend before the prom so I wouldn't have to take her. I figured my only choice was to break up with her rather than face the humiliation of not being able to get a suit for myself or a corsage for her. Of course, after the prom was over, I begged my way back into her life.)

At a fund-raiser for a school project in Ghana: from left, President and CEO of Black Entertainment Television Bob Johnson, actor Leon (front), comedian Michael Coylar, me, Denzel Washington, boxing promoter Butch Lewis, and president and CEO of Odyssey Services Fareed Ahmed.

A few days after I stopped going to school, several of my teachers came to see my grandmother. "We can't lose this young man," they told her. "He's got to stay in school. We think he shows a lot of promise."

My grandmother was shocked that I had been playing hooky, and I expected her to be terribly angry at me. But when she and my teachers finally understood why I'd left school, they came up with a solution. Those teachers gave me their husbands' hand-me-down clothes. One man was six-foot-six, which meant I had to wear his jackets with the sleeves rolled up and fix his pants so they didn't hang down too long and I wouldn't trip over the cuffs.

I'm not exaggerating when I say that those teachers at Manassas High School saved my life. They believed in me, and they taught me to believe in myself. It was there that I learned the power of an education, there that I finally understood that literacy is the real key to freedom, to undoing the shackles of oppression. It used to be against the law to teach black slaves to read and write, so I've always considered it the key to freedom. Education breaks down the barriers that hold you back from realizing your dreams. It lets you push through the limits people place on you.

It's important to realize that most kids who drop out of school aren't looking to take the easy way out. Most of the time, it's because they don't have decent clothes to wear or because they don't know how to study properly and they're afraid their teachers and classmates will think they're dumb. The people who pull these children back into school, who volunteer and tutor and teach, they are the real heroes in this world. Convincing a child that he can learn, showing him that education is a way out of a bad situation, can help persuade a dropout to return to class.

One of the lessons my teachers taught me was that my raggedy condition was temporary. If I was willing to make the commitment to stay in school, they said, I could make money and change my condition. Everybody's not going to be a millionaire, they added, but we believe you can grow up to make a decent living and have pride in your work. An education is the key to being your own boss, to being in charge of your own life. It's a lesson I passed down to my own kids: Finish school and do something with your life. I didn't tell them what to do, just encouraged them to do something, to make a contribution to the world, to take responsibility for the good of the community.

With Cicely Tyson at my Christmas party fund-raiser, Club Carbon, New York, 1998.

In 1993, those words came back to me—and I took responsibility. My friend Reverend Al Freddie Johnson came to see me when I was working in Los Angeles. He asked me to come down to Compton to see his literacy project in action. I visited him there and met some of the people whose lives his program was helping to change. One guy had been in a gang, another had been living in the street. Everywhere I turned, I heard those kinds of stories and talked to kids who were all "ex"— ex-homeless, ex–gang members, ex–drug addicts.

What I saw was just astounding, and I asked Reverend

Johnson how I could get involved in the work he was doing. But before I could get the words out of my mouth, he turned and asked me if I would become the international spokesperson for the World Literacy Crusade. He didn't have to ask me twice. I jumped at the chance.

I started going all over the world, speaking about the need for literacy and opening programs in many other cities. The need for these programs was undeniable. Reverend Johnson started the project

With singer Mary Wilson.

because he saw firsthand that the problems of the inner cities—poverty, drug addiction, homelessness, and violence—were linked to illiteracy. Where illiteracy was high, so was the crime rate.

L. Ron Hubbard wrote that the one thing we all have in common is the urge to survive, and education is the best way I know to help people not only survive but thrive in their communities. An educated person can be so much more than he was—more productive, more independent, a more ethical human being. Altering this one fact of life produces a ripple effect—and gives everyone involved a second chance.

When I speak on behalf of these literacy programs, I simply say: When a person can't read, it's as if he is lost in a foreign country. The letters of the alphabet look like meaningless squiggles; they may as well be hieroglyphics. An illiterate person feels locked out, angry, with few choices in life.

But education levels the playing field and changes the way a person relates to the world. Everything about him changes, including his ethics, and he has a fair chance—to reach for prosperity, to rise in life, even to achieve prominence. Anything is possible once he knows how to read.

My Ghana Project grew out of the World Literacy Crusade. I've been going to Africa since 1978, but I didn't visit Ghana, West Africa, until 1992, with my friend Dionne War-wick. We visited slave dungeons and talked to the people there. I was moved by what I saw and heard; it totally changed my life. I felt I had to do something to connect with the people of the continent. I started giving speeches at Black Expos, encouraging African-Americans to go to Africa, urging them to get involved and interact with the African people—socially, culturally, or through economic assistance.

A princess from Ghana named Asie Ocansey heard one of my talks. She was impressed that an American was so supportive of her country and such a goodwill ambassador. She contacted her father, who suggested that they honor me in some way. In fact, they asked me if I wanted to be a king. (Who wouldn't say yes, right?) I traveled back to Ghana, and in a memorable ceremony, I was made a king of an area called Ada, which is about a one-and-a-half-hour drive east of Accra, the capital. I renewed my commitment to help in the development of the area. It was the fulfillment of a dream.

I have come to realize that it takes more than just money and good intentions to help people. Education is clearly linked to progress and development, and that is where I am putting my efforts—including a project closer to home and close to my heart.

Last year, my old school, Manassas High School in North Memphis, Tennessee, celebrated its one hundredth anniversary. I had gone to that school and the lower school nearby

Being honored at a local festival in Ghana, 1998.

since the fourth grade. It was great to go back. Few things about the school had changed in forty years, but everything looked so small and decrepit.

I remember walking those halls between classes, going up and down the stairs all day. I can even see the kids during recess on the playground. The auditorium where I first messed around on the piano—and got chased off—is no longer there, and the school doesn't have a true music department anymore. In fact, I learned at the reunion that the school that saved my life, the place that, culturally and spiritually, made me feel rich in the midst of poverty, was slated to be demolished.

I hope we don't lose this important piece of our past. Manassas was the only black school in the city of Memphis, and the original building was built by slaves. I've been crusading to save the building, which I feel symbolizes a vital piece of our history. But even if I don't win the

My marker at Manassas High School.

battle to preserve the school as it was, I felt it was important to raise my voice on the subject.

I hope that with the help of the Isaac Hayes Foundation and others, we can help sustain what that school started and has meant to generations of Memphis kids. I want it to look like a college campus, a true citadel of learning, with a performing-arts department, plus premed, prelaw, and a great athletic program, too. It wouldn't just be for black kids but open to everyone. We'd be preserving the name and the heritage of the school, because our kids need to know our history, to have something to look back on with pride. I'm determined to keep the name alive and to make sure the story is known.

The state of Tennessee bestows markers, for the most part posthumously, to Tennesseeans it wishes to honor. There are three living recipients: Rufus Thomas, myself, and a country-western singer. Rufus put his marker on Beale Street. I asked that mine be placed at my alma mater. I hope that marker will continue to stand as an example to the kids of Memphis. Its simple message: You can study and make it, the way Isaac Hayes did.

Jammin' to the Barbecue Beat

Heart & Soul Heart & Soul Heart & Soul Heart & Soul Heart & Soul Heart & Soul Heart & Soul

Johnny Vanucci's Filet Mignon

Even when I wasn't writing down recipes, I used to pay close attention to how really good food was prepared. Back when I was in high school, I spent a year as a short-order cook at a Memphis restaurant called Vanucci's. One of the most popular dishes on the menu was filet mignon, prepared by the head of the family himself. This is how Johnny did it back then, and it's still a terrific way to serve this special cut of beef! *Serves 4*

4 slices bacon, boiled briefly
4 4-ounce filets mignons
Toothpicks
Salt to taste

Ground black pepper to taste
2 tablespoons plus 1 teaspoon butter
¼ cup red wine
1 tablespoon minced shallots

Wrap 1 slice of bacon around the outside of each filet and secure with toothpicks. Season the filets with salt and pepper.

Heat a large skillet over medium heat; melt 2 tablespoons butter and cook filets to desired doneness, about 3 minutes on each side, depending on thickness.

Remove filets to a plate and deglaze the hot pan with red wine, scraping the bottom of the pan to loosen any browned bits. Add the shallots and cook, stirring, until softened, about 1 minute. Add the remaining 1 teaspoon butter and stir into the wine to make a sauce. (Do not boil.)

Return the filets to the pan and warm through in the sauce.

Debbie Allen and Norm Nixon's Apple-Smoked Filet Mignon with Ginger-Snapped String Beans

Most people know Debbie Allen from movies like *Fame* and Norm Nixon as a legendary basketball player with the Los Angeles Lakers. This husband-and-wife team loves to entertain. Here's a recipe they both enjoy, a special meal that is both down-home and sophisticated in its flavors and preparation.

Serves 2

1 tablespoon balsamic vinegar
½ teaspoon sea salt
½ teaspoon freshly ground black pepper
1 Granny Smith apple, thinly sliced
1 tablespoon olive oil
2 4-ounce filets mignons
2 slices apple-smoked bacon or turkey bacon
Toothpicks

GINGER-SNAPPED STRING BEANS
1 cup peanut oil
1 handful long string beans (at least 20)
1 roasted red pepper, thinly sliced
3 julienne strips fresh gingerroot
¼ teaspoon salt

For the filets mignons: In a medium glass bowl, combine vinegar, salt, pepper, apple, and oil and mix well. Add the filets and rub with the marinade. Cover and refrigerate at least 6 hours.

Preheat oven to 325 degrees. Heat a medium ovenproof skillet over high heat and add the filets. (Reserve the apples from the marinade.) Sear filets 10 seconds on each side and remove to a plate. Wrap a bacon strip around the outside of each filet and secure with toothpicks. Roast 10 minutes. Place the marinated sliced apples over the filets and roast 10 to 15 minutes or to the desired doneness. Serve filets with their juices.

While filets cook, prepare beans: In a medium skillet, heat peanut oil over high heat. Add string beans and cook 3 minutes. Drain on paper towels.

Drain oil from skillet and add the beans, red pepper, ginger, and salt. Mix well. Serve with the filets mignons.

Chef's Salisbury Steak with Luv Gravy

What makes this dish so good is starting with really fresh chopped steak. That, and making your gravy the old-fashioned way instead of using gravy from a jar or can. (Not to say that I've never done it in a pinch, but this home-style gravy is surprisingly easy—and well worth the effort.) When seduction is on the menu, my character of Chef from *South Park* would serve this dish to win the lady over!

Serves 2 to 4

½ cup all-purpose flour
¼ teaspoon dried sage
Sea salt to taste
Ground black pepper to taste
4 5-ounce "steaks" of lean ground round

About ⅓ cup safflower or canola oil
1 cup chopped yellow onions
½ cup spring water
⅓ cup milk

Place the flour, sage, salt, and pepper in a paper bag and shake to mix. Working with one steak at a time, shake in bag until completely coated with the flour mixture. Shake off the excess flour and reserve for the gravy.

Pour oil into a large skillet to a depth of ⅛ inch and heat over medium-high heat. Add steaks and cook until browned, 3 to 5 minutes on each side. Drain steaks on paper towels and set aside.

Pour off all but 1 tablespoon of the oil from the skillet. Add onions and cook over medium heat until very brown. Spread the flour-coating mixture over the bottom of the pan and stir until browned. Slowly add the spring water, stirring until it begins to boil. Add the milk, stirring constantly, until the mixture steams.

Simmer the steaks in the gravy for about 5 minutes. Cover, turn off the heat, and let steaks stand for a few minutes to allow the meat to absorb the flavors of the gravy.

Josephina's Meat Loaf

I haven't yet eaten everything on the menu at Josephina's, one of my favorite New York restaurants, but I'm doing my best! Not only is the food really good; it's all organic, so you're ensuring good health at the same you're enjoying every bite. A slice of this delicious meat loaf has only 307 calories.

Serves 8

Canola oil cooking spray
3 tablespoons finely chopped garlic
3 tablespoons finely chopped shallots
3 tablespoons finely chopped celery
2 pounds extra-lean ground beef
3 egg whites, lightly beaten
½ cup low-sodium, fruit juice–sweetened
    ketchup
¼ cup low-sodium soy sauce

3 tablespoons finely chopped fresh parsley
2 tablespoons Worcestershire sauce
1 tablespoon finely chopped fresh oregano
1 tablespoon finely chopped fresh tarragon
1 tablespoon Tabasco sauce
1 teaspoon ground coriander
¼ teaspoon ground black pepper
Sea salt to taste

Preheat oven to 375 degrees.

Grease a large nonstick skillet with canola cooking spray and heat pan over medium flame. Add the garlic, shallots, and celery and sauté until softened, 4 to 5 minutes. Transfer to a large bowl. Add the beef, egg whites, ketchup, soy sauce, parsley, Worcestershire sauce, oregano, tarragon, Tabasco, coriander, pepper, and salt. Mix gently but thoroughly and place in a nonstick loaf pan. Bang the bottom of the pan on top of the counter to be sure that the mixture is packed firmly in the pan.

Bake until meat loaf is cooked through, about 40 minutes. Let cool for 15 minutes before slicing.

John Travolta's Hamburger Royale with Cheese

I got to know John Travolta when I was living in California. I liked his personal philosophy when it came to food, particularly his favorite splurge. He told me once, "For the finest cheeseburger, start with the finest ingredients." This dish will demonstrate just how right he is!

Serves 2

½ pound ground beef tenderloin, formed into
   2 patties
4 slices finest-quality cheddar cheese
2 homemade hamburger buns, split

2 tablespoons Russian dressing
4 leaves fresh lettuce
4 slices juicy, ripe tomato

Heat a grill pan. Cook burgers to your taste—I like them medium-rare to rare.

Put 2 slices cheese on top of each hamburger, cover, and cook for 1 more minute to melt the cheese. Place each cheeseburger on an open bun and spread on the Russian dressing.

Add lettuce and tomato and eat the burgers while they're hot.

Hall's Picnic

Every summer when my sister Willette and I were growing up, my grandparents would take us to the Hall's Picnic in Sommerville, Tennessee. The picnic was an all-day, all-night food festival put on by the Masons, a fraternal group associated with the local church, on whose grounds the event was held.

Elaborate preparations began the night before, when the men all worked together to dig a huge pit in the ground. Into the pit they'd lower a whole hog that had been cleaned, spiced, and stuffed in the cavity with onions and other aromatic vegetables. The hog was wrapped in a kind of sackcloth, which the men dampened with water, before putting the hog in the pit. Then they'd fill the pit with hot stones and coals, and finally they'd pack it with dirt. The hog would roast, smoldering, overnight in the earthen oven.

The next day, the men would dig the pig out and put it on a spit, where it would keep turning all day. Every so often, people would mop the pig with barbecue-sauce-soaked rags on sticks, which they kept dipping into a huge bucket of sauce. By about two in the afternoon, you could smell the sweet pork for miles around. When the pig was done, we'd stand there with our plates held out, waiting for just the pieces we wanted.

There was no charge for attendance at the picnic, but you paid for the food you wanted, including the barbecue sandwiches. Some enterprising folks set up food stalls to sell chicken sandwiches, spaghetti, coleslaw, or fried catfish. They'd yell, "Get your buffalo fish sandwich," or "Get your soft drink here!" The soft drinks were stored in these huge washtubs. They'd first put ice in the bottom, then pile in the bottles of soda, then cover the bottles with ice. Sometimes we'd stick our hands in the icy water just to see how cold we could stand it!

Throughout the day, there'd be people cranking ice cream makers while some of the men played horseshoes and carnival folks ran games and picture-taking booths. It felt like an enormous family reunion. Even if they moved away from Fayette County, people always came back each summer for the Hall's Picnic.

Because my grandparents were born in Sommerville, I had relatives up there. So many, in fact, it seemed like I was related to the entire county! We stayed with our cousins, but some people from out of town slept in their cars, which were parked in a long line stretching way down the road from the church. I remember one visit, after we'd been living in Memphis for a while, that convinced me I'd become a city kid. Some of my cousins took me swimming in a nearby pond. The water was murky, and when I felt something squiggly around my feet, I didn't wait to find out what it was. I just said, "No more, I'm gone!" and I got out of that pond real fast!

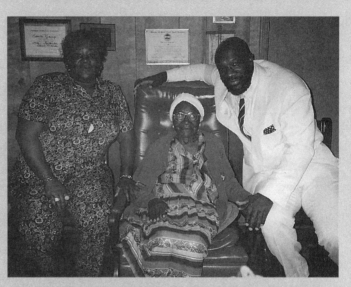

With my sister Willette Rankin and grandmother
Rushia Wade in Memphis, 1991.

The picnic would go on late into the night. By the time the sun went down, the whole area was lit up, illuminated by soda pop bottles with rag wicks dipped in kerosene strung together with wire from tree to tree like Japanese lanterns. There was music everywhere you turned. I remember the sound of a fife-and-drum corps performing marches, and the endless rhythms of a snare drum and bass drum echoing back and forth. Folks played guitar and sang the blues while the grown-ups would gather nearby and listen, drinking peach brandy or Muscadine wine. A few even brought their own moonshine. There must have been a few hundred people there most nights, arriving by dusty car or in trucks or mule-drawn wagons.

I remember, years later, driving up there in my first car, a used 1965 Ford Fairlane with a yellow body and a black vinyl top. I was in my twenties by then, married with children. The place didn't look the same as I remembered it. The food was as good as always, but the picnic didn't seem as big or boisterous or as much fun. I figured my days of going to the Hall's Picnic were over, but I knew I'd always keep the good memories of times gone by.

Super Bowl Sunday Baked Ham
with Beer-Based Glaze

Baking a ham is usually considered "special-occasion" cooking. It takes a lot of work and hours in the oven to get that perfect centerpiece for a holiday feast. But if you'd rather eat ham more often than not, start with meat that has already been precooked. The pleasure is in this sweet-spicy glaze that tastes far more complicated than it is to prepare.   *Serves 4 to 6*

1 precooked ham
1 12-ounce can of your favorite beer
1½ cups dark brown sugar

3 tablespoons balsamic vinegar
1 tablespoon dry mustard
Whole cloves

Preheat oven to 350 degrees.

Place the ham in a roasting pan and pour all but 2 tablespoons of the beer on top. Bake until cooked through, about 1 hour, basting occasionally with pan juices.

In a small bowl, mix reserved beer with the brown sugar, vinegar, and mustard to form a nice smooth paste. Remove the ham from oven and score the fat diagonally in two directions to form a diamond pattern. Spread the paste over the ham and stud with whole cloves.

Bake ham until it is well glazed, basting with drippings, about 40 minutes longer.

Marinated Boston Butt

This is one of the recipes I used to make back when I was just starting out in the world, right after high school. I'd just gotten married and was still living in Memphis. I loved cooking this dish for my wife and her family—and they loved eating it as much as I liked to make it! The cooking time depends on the size of the Boston butt and whether you bone and tie the meat. (By the way, the butt is actually a shoulder cut of pork, not the rear end, as you might think.)

Serves 4 to 6

1 5-to-7-pound Boston butt (bone-in or
    boneless and tied)
1 6-ounce can frozen apple juice concentrate,
    defrosted, plus ½ can water
1 cup apple cider vinegar

½ cup pickling spices
1½ teaspoons brown sugar
1 teaspoon ground Jamaican allspice
1 teaspoon chopped fresh cilantro
1 teaspoon dried basil

In a saucepan, combine the apple juice, water, vinegar, pickling spices, brown sugar, allspice, cilantro, and basil and mix well. Heat to boiling, simmer for 10 minutes and let cool.

Using a fork, pierce holes in the Boston butt and place in a large roasting pan. Pour the marinade on top. Cover and refrigerate overnight, turning occasionally.

Preheat oven to 350 degrees. Cover the butt and roast until cooked through, about 4 hours (depending on the size), basting with the marinade. Uncover the last 30 minutes to allow the glaze to brown.

Wendell Price

I first met my good friend chef Wendell Price at the Black Film Festival in Acapulco, Mexico, and we hit it off right away. He says it's because we have so much in common—besides "great taste in women." We both enjoy what he calls "down-home mama's cooking." He likes to say that he adds a little Cajun flavor to my hot buttered soul, and once you taste his recipes for the stars, I think you'll agree. (Check out his Chilled Collard Green Salad and Quick Salmon Penne.)

Wendell sees his role this way: "Celebrities living the good life always seem to want to go back to their roots, one way or another. That's where I come in. I incorporate their childhood food cravings into dishes that reflect today's chic, health-conscious style of eating."

It's a real pleasure cooking and sharing stories with Wendell, who has said he looks up to me as he would a father. For my part, I love the energy and innovation he brings to his food creations.

Just like me, Wendell's got his own website, so if you want to learn more about him, visit www.chefwendell.com.

With Pearlie Biles and Chef Wendell Price at a taste-testing for Cooking with Heart & Soul.

Lu's Chopped BBQ Pork

Pearlie introduced me to Lu Willard quite a few years ago. Lu listened to my visions of a diamond piano watch, and as a jeweler she helped me make that vision a reality. We became fast friends and have remained so over time. We also share a love of cooking and entertaining, which we've done together with Pearlie on occasion. Here's a recipe that will comfortably serve a houseful of hungry relatives and friends. Heat and serve this on your favorite bread or bun with my Memphis Magic barbecue sauces (see the back of the book) and my 24-Hour Coleslaw (page 146).   *Serves 4 to 6*

1 3- to 4-pound pork shoulder
Salt to taste
Pepper to taste
1 cup apple cider vinegar

⅓ cup brown sugar
3 tablespoons minced garlic
Crushed red pepper flakes to taste

Preheat oven to 350 degrees. Wash pork shoulder and pat dry with paper towels. Sprinkle the meat with salt and pepper and rub well. Place meat in a roasting pan and bake until falling off the bone, about 3½ hours.

Remove meat from the pan and chop into pieces. Drain the grease from the pan. Add the apple cider vinegar to the pan and heat to boiling on the stovetop, scraping the browned bits from the bottom of the pan.

Return the meat to the pan and add the brown sugar, garlic, and pepper flakes. Toss to mix well. Refrigerate at least 2 hours and heat through before serving.

A&R Bar-Be-Que

Growing up in the South, you learn that barbecue isn't just a meal; it's a ritual, a celebration of food and family that can last for hours. There are probably as many ways of making barbecue as there are southern cooks, and as many secret sauces that are passed down from one generation to the next. I've always loved eating barbecue, and I've passed that love on to my kids and my friends. But because I don't often have time to do my own barbecuing, I get my "fix" at my favorite restaurants.

Whenever I am in Memphis, I make sure to stop by A&R Bar-Be-Que, which has some of the best barbecue in the world. (Some might say it's the only place to eat barbecue!) The restaurant was founded in 1983 as a takeout place by Andrew Pollard, a friend of mine who once made barbecue for company at home using a round foot tub with a stove rack on top. Andrew started his business with only two thousand dollars, most of it borrowed from his parents, and a hundred fifty more borrowed for supplies and meats from his brother the day before the restaurant opened, and just one and a half employees (the one being himself and the half a part-time helper).

In his first year, he grossed about thirty-five thousand dollars. Since then, the business has taken on some twenty more employees and has added a seating area for more than seventy-five people as well as a catering service.

Andrew's secrets to success are:

With Andrew Pollard, owner of Memphis's A&R Bar-Be-Que, 1999.

- A cup of hard work
- A pint of consistency
- A quart of good-quality products
- And a heap of faith in God!

A&R Bar-Be-Que Spaghetti

Doesn't this sound like a dish fit for the King? There is no place in the world for barbecue like A&R Bar-Be-Que on Elvis Presley Boulevard in Memphis, and they were kind enough to share their recipe for this outrageous but great-tasting dish. If you're such a fan of barbecue that you could happily eat it every day, here's a way to make spaghetti night a barbecue treat never to be forgotten!

Serves 6

4 cups spaghetti sauce
2 cups barbecue sauce
1 tablespoon chili powder
2 tablespoons brown sugar

½ pound chopped cooked barbecued pork or beef
1 pound spaghetti, cooked, hot

In the top of a double boiler set over boiling water, combine the spaghetti sauce, barbecue sauce, chili powder, and brown sugar and cook over low heat, stirring occasionally, for 30 minutes.

Add the cooked barbecued pork or beef to the sauce mixture, cover, and cook 30 minutes longer.

Pour the barbecue and sauce over the spaghetti and serve.

A&R Bar-Be-Que Pork
Shoulder Sandwich

Depends on who you ask, of course, but some will tell you that the secret of barbecue is all in the cut of meat. Others will insist that it's the depth of the pit or the heat of the coals, or that it's all in the timing. I'm willing to agree with all those points of view, and I'd add that the sauce matters in a big way. When I can, I buy sauce directly from my first-choice Memphis restaurant, but you can use your local favorite if that's what you've got on hand!

1 3- to 4-pound pork shoulder
A&R Bar-Be-Que Sauce, heated

Sandwich buns, toasted
Coleslaw

Place the pork shoulder, fat- or skin-side down, on a grill rack over a very hot pit. Cook for 5 hours. Turn and cook until the shoulder reaches an internal temperature of 180 degrees in the thickest part when tested with a meat thermometer, about 3 hours longer.

Remove the pork shoulder from the pit, and pull off the meat as you need it. You may leave meat to pull or chop it. Take large toasted bun, pour hot sauce over meat, and add coleslaw. This makes a delicious, finger-licking sandwich.

A & R Bar-Be-Que Ribs

Never made your own barbecue ribs because you figured you couldn't make them taste as good as your favorite barbecue joint? Whether you're cooking with A&R sauce or my Memphis Magic sauces, or your own favorite, here's what you need to know to produce outstanding ribs.

3 to 4 pounds spareribs
Barbecue sauce

Prepare barbecue grill.

Remove the skin from the rib bones and grill the ribs, bone side down, until browned. (Make sure the ribs are not directly over the fire.) Turn the ribs and cook on other side until they are browned and tender. The cooking should be very slow and take about 2 hours. Remove ribs from barbecue and slather with barbecue sauce. Return to grill and cook an additional 30 minutes. Mm, mm, good!

Slaughtering Hogs

Everyone in our community always pitched in to help one another when help was needed. In church or from a passerby, you'd hear that a neighbor was going to put a new room on his house. No invitation was necessary—we'd all just show up to help him out. It was all "word of mouth" in the country when I was a boy. We had no telephones, no cars, no electricity. If someone was slaughtering a hog or killing a young calf for veal, neighbors would all join in to get the job done.

I remember that hog-killing time was usually one of the coldest days of the year, because nature was our freezer and we didn't want the meat to spoil before it was salted down and cured. It's true what they say, too: We used everything but the oink—pig's feet, the head, even the nose (or snout, as we called it), the tail, *everything*. First, they would quarter the pig and remove the various parts. We kids had a lot of fun playing with bits and pieces of the animal. We liked to take a pipe stem, put it into the bladder of the pig, and blow it up like a balloon. The ladies got the big, black three-legged kettles going. The kettles sat on bricks with a fire burning underneath, and the women would cut up the pork rind with a little fat and make cracklings. Delicious, with little streaks of lean meat and lots of fat—cholesterol city! Oh, the meat would smell so good cooking. As it cooked, the women drained the grease off and poured it into cans, so it could be used for shortening later on.

Then everything—the cracklings, the lard— would be stored in the smokehouse. We'd add the cracklings to cornbread to make what we called crackling bread. Mama would make sausages for the neighbors who helped us out with the slaughter. She'd get out the grinder and add herbs and spices to the meat along with peppers and sage. Once the sausages were made, she'd hang them in the smokehouse to cure. We'd pickle the pig's feet, which were considered a country delicacy. If you've never eaten them, let me warn you: your hands will feel like they're covered with glue! That's why they use pigs' feet to make glue, because they are so naturally sticky you can't pull your fingers apart. Oh, sure, you might start out using a fork and knife, but before long you'd wind up with that hog foot in your mouth and glue on your hands!

My grandfather liked to eat pig brains with his eggs. Everything but the oink, remember? There was even something called Rocky Mountain oysters, which were hog testes. I'll always remember my mama cooking up the pig's private parts because they had a very pungent smell. I once asked her, "Granny, what's that?"

She said, "You don't want to eat that, son." (But my grandfather let me taste it, and I liked it. Hard to describe the flavor, but it was good.) Another part that I liked was the liver, but I just couldn't eat the tongue.

On New Year's Eve it was considered good luck for the coming year to eat black-eyed peas and hog's head. You put the whole head in the pot and boiled it with the peas. I loved the pig ears. They were crunchy because of the cartilage; we called it gristle, and I gobbled it down. Nothing was wasted; nothing was thrown away. (I almost can't believe how much pork we all loved to eat back in those days, with no concern about potential health risks. Now, we only enjoy it in moderation—and it's still good.)

Splish-Splash! Seafood in and out of the Shell

Delta Fried Catfish

In a perfect world, you'd be eating your catfish only a little while after catching them, and they'd be so fresh they'd practically be jumping around the skillet! Well, most of us get our catfish already filleted at the market, but if you happen to buy it whole (or get some freshly caught from a friend), you can use the whole fish, head to tail, as long as it's cleaned and scaled.

Serves 2 to 4

2 cups yellow cornmeal
1 teaspoon Old Bay seasoning
1 teaspoon dry mustard
1 teaspoon salt

1 teaspoon pepper
4 catfish fillets
Vegetable oil for frying

In a large, shallow bowl, combine cornmeal, Old Bay seasoning, mustard, salt, and pepper and mix well. Coat each fillet with the seasoned cornmeal and shake off any excess.

Pour oil into a large skillet to measure ⅛ inch deep and heat until hot over medium-high heat. Cook the catfish until golden brown and crisp, turning once, being careful to maintain the oil temperature so that it is hot enough to cook the fish through but not so hot that the outside cooks too much.

Fried Red Snapper

A smart cook doesn't mess with what's already outstanding, so when you've got really fresh fish, a simple preparation like this one is all you need. *Serves 4*

Yellow cornmeal seasoned with Old Bay seasoning and salt and pepper

4 red snapper fillets
Vegetable oil for frying

Put the seasoned cornmeal on a plate. Dredge each fillet in the cornmeal, shaking off the excess.

Film the bottom of a frying pan with the vegetable oil. When the oil is hot, add the snapper fillets. Fry until the outside is crisp and the flesh flakes when touched with a fork.

Salmon Baked in Foil

Salmon is one of my favorite kinds of fish, and this recipe is a real favorite. It's healthy, it tastes great, and it's as easy to make for one person as it is for ten. The blend of spices is key, of course, as well as keeping a close eye on how fast your broiler flame browns the top.

Serves 4

Pinch of Spike seasoning
Pinch of Chinese five-spice powder
Pinch of curry powder
Pinch of Old Bay seasoning
Pinch of dried tarragon
Pinch of dried sweet basil

Pinch of Jamaica allspice
4 4- to 6-ounce salmon fillets
4 tablespoons water or dry white wine
4 pinches of ground cumin
4 teaspoons soy sauce

Preheat oven to 400 degrees. Cut 4 pieces of aluminum foil each large enough to enclose 1 salmon fillet. In a bowl, mix the Spike, spice powder, curry powder, Old Bay seasoning, tarragon, basil, and allspice and sprinkle over the center of each piece of foil, dividing evenly. Top with a salmon fillet; sprinkle each with 1 tablespoon water or wine, a pinch of cumin, and 1 teaspoon soy sauce.

Fold up the corners of the foil to enclose the fish. Tightly seal the packets and place on a baking sheet. Bake packets for 10 minutes.

Preheat the broiler.

Carefully open the top of each packet and broil 3 to 5 minutes. The salmon should be slightly browned on top, but be careful not to overcook it.

Serve with my Sautéed Spinach (see page 48).

John Singleton's White Fish
with Crabmeat Stuffing

He was the youngest person ever to be Oscar nominated for Best Director (for *Boys N the Hood*), and recently it's been my great pleasure to work with John Singleton on the remake of *Shaft*. This is a terrific way to prepare any kind of white-fleshed fish—sole, flounder, halibut, or cod are just some of the possibilities.

Serves 4

2 tablespoons olive oil
1 red onion, diced
1 shallot, minced
1 clove garlic, minced
1 tablespoon Creole seasoning plus
    additional for sprinkling
1 teaspoon freshly ground black pepper
½ teaspoon curry powder
½ teaspoon paprika
Pinch of sea salt

1 pound lump crabmeat, picked over
1 egg yolk
2 tablespoons plain dry bread crumbs
1 teaspoon chopped fresh parsley
1 chive, minced
1 teaspoon fresh lemon juice
1 4-pound whole white fish, cleaned, leaving
    head and tail intact
2 strips bacon
Toothpicks

In a large skillet, heat the oil over medium heat. Add the onion, shallot, and garlic and sauté until onion is caramelized, about 15 minutes.

Add 1 tablespoon Creole seasoning, black pepper, curry powder, paprika, and salt; mix well and cook for 5 minutes. Remove pan from heat. Stir in the crabmeat, egg yolk, bread crumbs, parsley, and chives and let sit for 30 minutes.

Preheat oven to 375 degrees.

Rub lemon juice over the fish and sprinkle with Creole seasoning. Lay the fish on a greased baking sheet and open the cavity. Stuff with the crabmeat mixture, wrap bacon around fish and secure with toothpicks. Cover the baking sheet with aluminum foil.

Bake the fish for 20 minutes. Remove foil and cook until browned and cooked through, about 10 minutes longer.

This fish is especially delicious served with steamed asparagus.

Victoria Dillard's Halibut with Mango Chutney Sauce on Coconut Rice

S he's so good in the movies and on television, no one would expect the beautiful Victoria Dillard also to be a spectacular cook. But this recipe will persuade you just how talented one woman can be! Serve this to guests at a sunset barbecue—it's fast and tastes great.

Serves 2

MANGO-CHUTNEY SAUCE
1 mango, pitted, peeled, and diced
1 small onion, minced
¼ cup pineapple juice
1 tablespoon wine vinegar
1 tablespoon brown sugar
1 teaspoon chopped fresh cilantro
1 tablespoon ground Jamaican allspice
1 teaspoon cinnamon
1 teaspoon grated nutmeg

COCONUT RICE
1 cup Uncle Ben's rice
⅓ cup shredded coconut
1 teaspoon Chinese five-spice powder
2 6-ounce halibut fillets
Baby chives for garnish

For the chutney sauce, in a medium bowl, combine the mango, onion, pineapple juice, vinegar, brown sugar, cilantro, allspice, cinnamon, and nutmeg and mix well. Set aside.

For the coconut rice, in a small saucepan, cook the rice according to package directions. Mix the hot rice with the coconut and five-spice powder. Set aside and keep warm.

Grill the fish on a wire rack set over medium coals for 2 minutes on each side.

Serve fish over rice with the chutney. Garnish with baby chives. Enjoy.

Jamaican Jerk Fish

I've traveled many times down to the Caribbean, and I've become a real fan of Jamaican dishes prepared with a "jerk" sauce. Depending on the chef, jerk meats and fish can set your mouth on fire, or warm it up just enough. You can usually find jerk seasoning in most cities; if not, you can probably find a source for it on-line.

Serves 16 to 18

1 6-pound whole salmon, cleaned, gutted,
   and filleted
Juice of one lemon
3 tablespoons butter
1 to 2 cups salsa
2 cloves garlic, minced

Lawry's seasoned salt
Lemon pepper, salt free
Cajun seasoning
Dry jerk seasoning
Chopped scallions or garnish
1 recipe Spinach-Shrimp Stuffing (see below)

Wash fish and soak for approximately 20 minutes in at least one gallon of water mixed with lemon juice. Place half of the fish skin-side down on very heavy foil coated with non-stick spray. Top with Spinach-Shrimp Stuffing (see below). Place other half of fish skin-side up on top of mixture and dot fish with butter. Seal the foil very tightly and bake approximately 45 minutes. Drain and reserve drippings. In a small saucepan, heat the drippings, salsa, and a little each of the garlic, salt, lemon pepper, and Cajun and jerk seasoning. Pour over fish and garnish with scallions.

SPINACH–SHRIMP STUFFING
1 to 2 cups cooked shrimp
1 to 2 cups fresh spinach, washed and
   trimmed

½ teaspoon minced garlic
Pinch each of Lawry's seasoned salt, no-salt
   lemon pepper, Cajun seasoning, and jerk
   seasoning

In a large bowl, combine all the ingredients.

Tito Nieves's "I Like It Like That" Baked Crab Legs

I asked renowned salsa musician Tito Nieves to share his favorite way of preparing crab legs. The key to this simple but delicious preparation is using lots of fresh garlic, not the dried, minced kind you may have in your spice rack. As long as you and your guests are true garlic lovers, don't worry about using too much. Garlic loses some of its bite when it bakes, and besides, as long as everyone is having some, there's no worry about garlic breath! *Serves 2*

4 tablespoons butter
2 tablespoons minced garlic

1½ tablespoons bread crumbs
2 pounds snow crab legs

Preheat oven to 300 degrees.

In a small skillet, melt the butter over medium heat. Add the garlic and sauté until soft, about 5 minutes. Stir in the bread crumbs and sauté until toasted, about 3 minutes.

Spread the crab legs over a baking sheet and top with the bread crumb mixture. Bake crabs for 20 minutes.

Tastes fabulous and garlicky.

Dominique Jennings's Stuffed Colossal Shrimp with Saucy Étouffée

Here's a perfect recipe for a beautiful actress—and the rest of us, too! Dominique has appeared in *Sunset Beach* and *Fresh Prince of Bel-Air,* and she knows that sometimes one spectacular piece of seafood can satisfy.

Serves 3

SAUCY ÉTOUFFÉE
4 tablespoons butter
2 white onions, diced
2 green bell peppers, diced
1 celery stalk, finely chopped
1 clove garlic, minced
1 tablespoon chopped fresh parsley
1 cup seafood stock

5 tablespoons white wine
1 tablespoon fresh lemon juice
1 pound cleaned crawfish
1 teaspoon all-purpose flour
1 tablespoon paprika

Preheat oven to 325 degrees. Grease a small baking pan and set aside.

Make the Saucy Étouffée: In a medium saucepan, melt the butter over medium heat and add the onions, bell peppers, celery, garlic, and parsley and sauté until onions are caramelized, about 15 minutes. Stir in the stock, wine, and lemon juice and simmer until liquid has reduced, about 10 minutes. Add the crawfish and cook through, about 5 minutes. Blend in the flour and cook, stirring, until sauce is thickened. Add the paprika and simmer, stirring, for 15 minutes.

STUFFED SHRIMP
1 tablespoon butter
1 small onion, minced
1 clove garlic, minced
1 sprig parsley, minced
3 tablespoons white wine
1 cup lump crabmeat
⅓ cup cleaned crawfish
1 tablespoon bread crumbs

1 egg yolk
Pinch of sea salt
Pinch of ground white pepper
3 colossal shrimp, peeled, deveined, and
    butterflied
Chopped fresh thyme for garnish

To prepare the shrimp, in a large skillet, melt the butter over medium heat and sauté the onion, garlic, and parsley until the onion is soft, about 5 minutes. Add the wine and boil until almost evaporated. Stir in the crabmeat, crawfish, bread crumbs, egg yolk, salt, and pepper and mix well. Remove the pan from the heat.

Place the shrimp in the prepared baking pan and open up. Fill with the stuffing, mounding on top, and bake for 20 minutes. Serve on a plate of the Saucy Étouffée. Garnish with chopped fresh thyme.

Annette's Seafood Boil

This is one of my favorite one-pot meals—the classic crab boil made even more delicious by the addition of more seafood and some spicy sausage for good measure! This is a great meal to serve when friends come for dinner because all the prep work is done in advance, and you can be visiting while it boils away on the stove. *Serves 6 to 8*

1 gallon spring water
1 5-ounce package mild crab boil or shrimp spice
⅓ cup salt
1 lemon, quartered
16 small red potatoes
4 ears corn, cut into 3-inch pieces
4 carrots, peeled, cut into 2-inch pieces

2 white onions, thinly sliced
2 celery stalks, coarsely chopped
1 head garlic, peeled and broken into cloves
3 pounds crawfish
1 pound unpeeled shrimp
1 pound kielbasa sausage, cut into 2-inch pieces

In a large pot with a wire basket, combine water, crab boil, salt, and lemon and heat to boiling. Add the potatoes, corn, carrots, onions, celery, and garlic cloves and cook until vegetables are tender, about 10 minutes. Do not overcook.

Add crawfish, shrimp, and sausage. Cover and simmer for 10 to 12 minutes.

Lift the basket out of the pot. Remove vegetables, seafood, and sausage and serve.

Barbara Carey's Shrimp Creole

Creole-style cooking draws from many different traditions—the French who came to Louisiana before the American Revolution; the Choctaw Indians, who taught the settlers to use sassafras to thicken their soups and stews; African slaves, who added okra to many dishes; and later, the Spanish, who spiced things up even more. Miami is my second home, a place I love to visit often, and City Commissioner Barbara Carey is one of the reasons it's a great place to live.

Serves 2 to 4

2 tablespoons vegetable oil
2 cups peeled and deveined shrimp
1 cup chopped green bell pepper
½ cup minced onion
½ cup sliced celery
1 clove garlic, minced
½ 6-ounce can tomato paste

1½ cups water
¾ teaspoon salt
1 bay leaf
¼ teaspoon dried thyme leaves
⅛ teaspoon ground black pepper
Cooked white rice

In a large skillet, heat the oil over medium-high heat, add the shrimp, bell pepper, onion, celery, and garlic and sauté until fragrant, about 1 minute. Stir in the tomato paste and then the water and seasonings. Simmer until vegetables are softened, 10 to 12 minutes, stirring occasionally.

Serve over white rice.

I GOT MUSIC
ON MY MIND

ne of my most cherished memories is sitting on the front porch of our house in Covington, after working hard all day in the fields, and singing Negro spirituals with my family. Even now, so many years later, it's one of the times that comes to mind when I remember our days together in the country.

Music was always a part of my life from the very beginning. I came from a very musical family—my mother was a singer, my grandmother sang and played the piano, and well, my grandfather could sing loud, but that was about it. The first time I sang in public was in a church duet with my sister Willette when I was three years old. But it wasn't until I won a talent show sponsored by my high school in Memphis that I'd even thought about music as a career.

The tryouts for the talent show took place in the school auditorium. I was the last one to show up for the audition that night. They were about to shut down when I arrived, a little out of breath but determined. Miss Georgia Harvey, who was the school guidance counselor and in charge of the show, asked me, "What do you want to do?"

"I'm going to sing," I answered.

"Oh, yeah?" she said. "Well, get out there and sing, little boy."

I walked to the center of the stage and started singing Nat King Cole's "Looking Back." The auditorium was still full of kids talking and milling around, but the whole place got quiet. When I finished the song, all you could hear was the loud roar of the crowd shouting "Yeah!"

Miss Harvey jumped up and hugged me, then said, "What's your name, son? You're going to be in the show tomorrow!"

I was a little surprised by the intensity of everyone's reaction, but I was happy to make the cut. When I showed up the next day, the feeling was the same, only better.

"Y'all," Miss Harvey announced, "I've got a young man here who was the last contestant to audition last night. He walked in and said he wanted to sing." She gestured to me, and I must have looked like this raggedy scarecrow. She finished the introduction, saying, "I think y'all might like this young man."

That's me on the left, with other contestants at radio station WDIA's talent show, Memphis, 1958.

I started to sing "Looking Back" again, and the response was amazing. I tore the place up. *Tore it up.* They wanted me to sing an encore, but I didn't have anything else prepared.

I immediately became a school celebrity. I even started signing autographs and all the pretty girls swarmed around me. Usually the guys who played football and basketball got all the girls. But now it was my turn! I started getting all the girls I'd ever wanted. And the best thing was outdoing those basketball and football boys. See, they only have a girl for a season because their sport only lasts a few months, but I was getting girls all year round because I could sing all year round!

Then the older girls, the eleventh and twelfth graders, invited me to have lunch with them. I didn't have any money, but they said, "Oh, we'll buy you lunch, come sit with us."

That talent show was a turning point that changed my life. Before then, I'd dreamed of being a doctor, but now that I'd tasted success—and was getting all the girls—I wanted to be a musician.

Not long after that first talent show, I began joining

Stax Records, Memphis, 1972.
PHOTOGRAPH © ERNEST C. WITHERS PHOTOGRAPHER.

musical groups and singing all different kinds of music. I performed doo-wop with two groups, the Teen Tones and the Ambassadors. I sang gospel with the Morning Stars and blues with Calvin Valentine and the Swing Cats. To top it off, I was singing jazz in a local night-club, Curry's Club Tropicana. And all this while I was still in high school!

I won seven vocal music scholarships from colleges around the country— Mississippi, Florida, and Tennessee among them. But I didn't take any of them. After graduating from high school, I got married and my wife had a baby, so going to college just wasn't possible. I had to get a job.

And I took whatever jobs I could find at first. Some were better than others. The worst was working in a meatpacking house. It was so different from slaughtering hogs and cows in the country. You can't imagine the noise and the smell. After working there, I found it hard to eat meat for a long while. But I got through it by working on my music every chance I got. All during the time I had the job at the meatpacking house, I was writing songs and auditioning.

See, even though I had to work to put food on the table, I knew that I wanted a career in music. Most of all, I wanted to work for Stax Records, a black-oriented record company—a place so hot everyone wanted to work there. Musically, it was an exciting time to be in Memphis. The town was booming—Elvis Presley, of course, Jerry Lee Lewis, and

Rufus Thomas, who was Stax's first release, I think. Over the years, the roster included Otis Redding, Sam and Dave, Soul Children, the Mad Lads, Johnny Taylor, The Staple Singers, Booker T. and the MGs, William Bell, Carla Thomas, Albert King, and, later on, Isaac Hayes—but that's getting ahead of the story.

I recorded my first single in 1962, the year I graduated from high school, but it didn't sell anything. It was a nice tune called "Laura, We're on Our Go-'round," written by a lady named Patty Ferguson. I played it not too long ago on my radio program on KISS-FM up in New York. My voice in that song has a real pop sound—to a Neil Sedaka beat—but I was writing R&B. My greatest influences were Nat King Cole, Perry Como, and Tony Bennett. Their tunes were my tunes. So after "Laura" didn't hit, I went back to the drawing board.

Around that time I was a lead singer in various bands, and I'd taught myself how to play keyboards. I was performing at a place called the Southern Club, and I really learned to play by practicing every night on the job. As with so many other things in my life, I learned to do by doing.

It was through a friend, Floyd Newman, who was a baritone sax player, that I got into Stax Records. He was up for a record, and he brought me in to play with him. That did the trick, and I got a job at Stax as a sideman, or studio musician.

It was there that I met David Porter. Working as Hayes and Porter, we began writing songs. Well, initially we were just writing songs, but before long we were writing *hit* songs. My first check for writing came for "How Do You Quit Someone You Love?" sung by Carla Thomas, and the next for a tune called "Can't See You When I Want To."

We were doing pretty well up to this point, and then we met Sam and Dave. We started writing for them—one hit after another: "Soul Man," "Hold On, I'm Coming," "You Don't Know Like I Know," and "When Something Is Wrong with My Baby." Working with Sam and Dave was the best. If the recording session was scheduled for the next day, they'd stay up with us all night while we were writing for them, eating junk food, smoking cigarettes, and drinking together long into the night.

By 1967, I got the opportunity to record again. It was not exactly the way I would have planned it, but one afternoon we were celebrating a birthday at the studio. Duck Dunn, the bass player for Booker T. and the MGs, and I absconded with two bottles of champagne and two hunks of cake and headed for the ladies' bathroom. We locked the door and sat there on the floor eating cake and drinking champagne. When we finally emerged, we were feeling no pain. Al Bell, who was then head of promotions at Stax, came up to me and said, "Ike, are you going to record?"

I replied, "Yeah!" and headed into the studio, not sure if he was serious. With the late Al Jackson on drums, Duck on bass, and me on keyboards, I said, "Y'all follow me, one, two, three . . ." We didn't rehearse—it was all impromptu. Al just let the tape roll. I segued one cut into the next, and if you listen to the album *Presenting Isaac Hayes,* you can tell.

We finished, and Al said, "Well, I think I got what I want."

I said, "Okay." Never thought about it again. Two weeks later, I get a call from the studio photographer. "What?" I asked when he called me.

"Yeah, we got an album on you," he said. I went to the photographer and took a really nerdy picture. In it, I'm wearing a tails, a top hat, and a cane. What did I know? At least the record wasn't a total flop. The critics liked it, and it sold a few copies, too.

I was working at Stax around the time that Dr. Martin Luther King was really challenging all Americans to question the status quo. He was a great inspiration to me. I "sat in" at segregated lunch counters in Memphis, and I marched when there was a rally or demonstration. At the last march, not long before Dr. King's assassination, things got out of control. The cops showered us with Mace and set dogs on the demonstrators. It was terrifying for all of us.

One day, during a time of racial strife and riots in town, Booker T., David, Steve Cropper, Duck, Al, and I were standing in front of the Stax studios. Some cops came around the corner, jumped out of their cars, and started swinging billy clubs at us, shouting "Get back in there!"

They tried to beat us off the street. We weren't loitering; we were simply standing there in front of a business establishment where we worked. But as a group of black men, we were a target they couldn't resist. After attacking us, they went into the snack bar across the street and beat people out of the place. These people were just in there eating, and the cops moved in for no reason and started beating them. Nobody was doing anything to provoke them, but that didn't matter at the time.

I remember when National Guardsmen were posted every few yards apart up and down the streets. A friend of mine was almost shot. We had gotten special permission from the city to work that night, because we had a session to do in the studio. Benny Mabone, who is now my road manager, stepped outside to get some fresh air, and one of the National Guardsmen—a young white kid—was scared to death and cocked his gun. Benny heard the *clack-clack* and threw himself on the ground, saying, "Don't shoot me, we got permission from downtown to be in the studio!" It was close. A nervous kid like that could have fired a round or two and killed Benny. That's how volatile the situation was.

Like everyone else, I vividly remember the day Dr. King was shot: April 4, 1968. I could have been at the Lorraine Motel when it happened. I was scheduled to have dinner with him that night—my first chance to sit down with a man who was such a hero and an inspiration to me. At the time, David and I were producing a record for Sam and Dave, and we needed to do some orchestration. A man called Toby played baritone saxophone with them on the road, and we needed a baritone sax for the record. So we flew Toby into Memphis and put him up at the Lorraine Motel, which was just off Beale Street. I had only one car, and my wife needed it that day. I called Toby and said, "I can't pick you up. You're going to have to get a taxi to the studio."

Then I took a taxi to the studio, too. When I got to Stax, everybody was standing around looking very weird. I asked, "Why the long faces?"

"You haven't heard?" somebody answered. "Martin Luther King just got shot down at the Lorraine Motel!" Toby and I looked at each other and knew how close we'd come to being there.

After the assassination, I was paralyzed by my hatred for white folks because they'd killed my leader, my future. *Our future.* For about a year I didn't do anything creatively. But I had to come to grips with everything I was feeling. I had to do *something.* I decided that the best way to honor Dr. King's memory was to be the best that I could be. I had to try to make a difference, try to influence people and bring real change to the world. I couldn't do that by sitting in a room, sulking and hating all the time.

So I went back to the studio. Dave and I started writing again, but we agreed there had to be some changes made. We started right there at Stax Records,

At the Lorraine Motel,
site of Martin Luther King Jr.'s assassination, 1972.

made them hire more black people. Since they were selling to a black audience, they needed to be represented by blacks. I was always up in the offices raising hell, but we changed a lot of the rules that year.

In the spring of 1969, I did an album called *Hot Buttered Soul* that started the ball rolling for me. The album has four tunes on it, two cuts on each side. I felt good about the album because I'd been able to have total freedom as an artist. At last, I got to do what I wanted to do, with a lot of control and *without* the effects of the champagne that had marked my first recording session.

I knew that the album captured me, but I didn't care if it was a commercial success or not. If it didn't hit, I didn't care, because I'd done what I wanted to do. But it did succeed, far beyond anyone's expectations. In just a short time it went platinum.

My first job performing as "Isaac Hayes" was in August of that year at the Masonic Temple in Detroit. I was touring for *Hot Buttered Soul* with my band, the Movement. A local disc jockey was the master of ceremonies for the concert, and I asked him, "Think they are going to like me?"

He said, "Hell, it's been sold out for two weeks in advance. What do you think?" I was still intimidated, but when I went out on stage that night, something happened. I realized right away that the mike wasn't right. I felt nervous but I said, "You all have got to excuse me, but I've got to adjust this mike." I got up from my stool and did just that, then sat back down and said, "Now we'll play."

The sensation of going out on stage was frightening at first, but then everybody applauded and I thought, "Oh God, they're expecting all kinds of stuff out of me—will they like what I do?" All these worries were racing through my head. But when I broke the ice by talking to them, boom, the fright went away. The tension was gone. When I started performing, it felt good. The band was grooving and pleasing the audience.

At the time I was wearing a floppy terry-cloth cap. I took the cap off and I heard the women scream. *Bald head.* I made a mental note. I realized they went for the bald-head look because that was the picture on the cover of *Hot Buttered Soul.* The audience's reaction helped me develop my onstage persona.

I started wearing chains because they were a sign of strength. To me, there was no deeper symbolism at first. Later I realized that here I was, a black man choosing to drape myself in chains. Sure, chains were sexy and all, but at one time, those chains meant bondage and slavery. Now chains were transformed to mean power and masculinity and virility. I felt as if I was having a constant, unspoken dialogue with my fans about who I was, and also about who they were and how they saw themselves in me.

Performing at Wattstax, Los Angeles, 1972.
PHOTOGRAPH © 1973 COLUMBIA PICTURES,
COURTESY STAX ARCHIVES (FANTASY, INC.).

(I am always honest with the audience. Be honest with them, and they will go with you wherever you want to take them. Some people get stagehands to do things onstage—Oh, don't touch that mike!—but I don't believe in that because it distances you from your audience. When they realize you are just like them, that you are down to earth, then you can connect with the audience on a deeper level. I've been like that with my audiences ever since. I talk to them—it brings me closer, and I enjoy it.)

After *Hot Buttered Soul,* I got the nod to do *Shaft.* Melvin Van Peebles, a great actor and director (and Mario's father), had just made a movie called *Sweet Sweetback's Baad-asssss Song.* He couldn't get any major company to distribute it, so he did it himself. He took the film to different cities and rented theaters to show it. Black audiences flocked to see it, and Hollywood took notice. Somebody finally got the idea that black folks buy tickets to the movies. So they thought, Let's do a movie with a black leading man, a black director, and a black composer. Someone got Stax into the mix, and because I was their biggest gun, they asked me to come out to California.

The Shaft *team at the NAACP Image Awards, 1972.*
From left, me, producer Joel Friedman, director Gordon Parks,
and actor Richard Roundtree.

We had a meeting at MGM with Jim Aubrey, the president of the studio. They told me what they wanted to do and asked if I was interested. I said I was but that I had never scored a movie. They told me not to worry about that because they could provide all the technical assistance I needed. But now that I found myself in Hollywood, I asked the producers if I could try out for the starring role. "Oh, yes, Mr. Hayes," they said, "we'll give you a chance to try out."

I went back home and started bragging to everybody I knew, "Hey, man, I'm going to try out for this movie called *Shaft*!" I'd already committed to do the music, but I was excited about getting the chance to act. A couple of weeks passed and a friend said to me, "Hey, what about that movie you're supposed to be trying out for, did they call you yet?"

"No, but they will," I replied. Well, they never did. So I called them. "Oh, Mr. Hayes, no one told you? They already cast the part with a guy named Richard Roundtree." I couldn't believe it—the part was gone! The part I wanted was gone!

Then they said, "You still have to do the music because you said you'd do it." "All right," I told them, but I was still very disappointed that I didn't even get to audition for the part.

Even though I was sorry not to be in front of the camera, too, the picture turned out to be a phenomenal success for me. I was nominated for two Academy Awards and eight Grammys, which was a record for Grammy nominations at the time.

We all had a great time at the Grammys. Bobby Darin hosted the ceremony in New York, and I'd brought a big Memphis contingent with me—lots of family and friends—who got to see me win two Grammys. I also won an NAACP Image Award that year, but nothing was more exciting than the Oscars.

I can still remember hearing my name being announced at the Academy Award ceremony. I walked down the aisle, and when I got halfway across the stage, I saw Sammy Davis, Jr., backstage holding on to Joel Grey and saying, "I told you, I told you." Sammy had been a big help to me at the time, giving parties for me and helping me work Hollywood on behalf of the film.

Just like always, my grandmother never lost confidence in me. And on the night of the Academy Awards, I didn't even consider taking anybody else as my date. I'd prayed that God would keep her well so she could share in my success, and now, at last, I had the perfect opportunity.

My grandmother Rushia Wade and me returning to Memphis after the Academy Awards, 1972. PHOTOGRAPH © ERNEST C. WITHERS PHOTOGRAPHER.

We had such a wonderful time, I'll never forget any of it. She was eighty years old in 1972. I put her up at the Beverly Hilton because I wanted her to live in style while she was visiting Hollywood. By then, I had a home in Beverly Hills, a four-acre spread. We went out to the yard, which was beautifully landscaped, and I gave her the grand tour, including my bird sanctuary and the stables. Finally she said, "Mmmm, I never thought I'd live to see this day." I choked up, because I knew exactly what she meant. After all the years—the hard times, the menial work—her sacrifices and prayers had been rewarded.

I didn't want her to see the tears I couldn't hold back anymore. At that moment, I felt I was blessed, blessed that I could share my success with her. She was the lady who got me there, the one who kept me always grateful, always humble. She was my guiding light, helping me to stay clear of all the traps and vices.

I let her keep the Oscar. Then, about five years before she passed, she said, "You take this thing. I've had it long enough."

My grandmother was never really sick in her entire life. In 1997, I was down in the Caribbean when my niece called. "Mama's in the hospital," she told me. I asked what was wrong with her, and she said, "She's not eating. She stopped eating." I knew then that at one hundred and five years, she was ready to go. A couple of weeks later she died.

The pain I felt at her death was selfish, I knew, but I was grateful that I had been able to take good care of her, and repay her, in a small way, for all those times she supported and encouraged me. "Don't worry," she'd say when the kids were teasing me or giving me a hard time. "They'll be jealous of what they don't have. Just keep living, keep living." Mama, as always, was right.

Over the Fire, into the Fryer: Chicken for Sunday and Any Day

Mama's Roasted Chicken

About every third Sunday in Covington, the preacher would come to our house for dinner, and Mama would always serve her roast chicken with all the trimmings. Even today, when I'm roasting a chicken, I experience a kind of flashback to those days, when we kids had to wait for him to finish his dinner before we could finally gobble down whatever was left. The waiting was almost more than we could bear!

Serves 4

The biggest chicken you can find
1 tablespoon dried sage
1 teaspoon garlic salt

Salt to taste
Pepper to taste
Cotton string

Preheat oven to 350 degrees.

Wash the chicken inside and out and pat dry with paper towels. Season the chicken inside and outside with the sage, garlic salt, salt, and pepper. Tie the legs together with cotton string.

Place the chicken in a roasting pan. Add water to the pan to a depth of about 1 inch and cover the pan with the lid.

Roast the chicken 20 minutes per pound, basting occasionally with drippings, until it is cooked through.

"Do the Funky" Fried Chicken

Making fried chicken is a competitive sport among southern cooks, who don't always want to share their special techniques for getting the skin spectacularly crisp and crunchy. Here's my secret: Make sure you keep the oil very hot, so the outside gets crisp while the inside cooks through. I think Rufus Thomas would gladly have pulled up a chair on a night this was being served.

Serves 2 to 4

2 cups all-purpose flour
1 tablespoon Creole seasoning
1 teaspoon Spike seasoning
Salt to taste

3 eggs
4 chicken parts (your favorite)
2 cups canola oil

In a paper bag, combine the flour, Creole seasoning, Spike, and salt and shake to mix. In a shallow bowl, beat the eggs. Dip chicken in the eggs, drain off the excess, and place in the seasoned flour in the bag. Shake until well coated. Shake off any excess flour mixture.

In a large skillet, heat the oil over medium to medium-high heat until it is hot. Fry the chicken, in batches, if necessary, so you don't crowd the pan. Turn the pieces occasionally while cooking, until the outsides are brown and crisp and the insides are cooked through. Keep the heat up but watch the chicken so it doesn't brown too quickly before it is done. Prick the chicken with a fork to ensure it is cooked. The juices should run clear, not pink.

Drain on paper towels. Serve hot.

Preacher for Dinner

Across the road from our house were a church and a school that shared grounds. The church was Southern Baptist, and the congregation met in a wooden-framed building that was the center of our community, the heart of our social life. The first time I sang in public was in that church. (It was a duet with my sister at Eastertime, and Mama played the piano. Willette got the tune wrong, and right in the middle of the song I stopped her and showed her how to sing it right.)

On some Sundays, the preacher would invite people to bring box lunches to church for a picnic after services. If a lady liked a particular man, she would bring him a box lunch so he could taste her cooking and decide whether or not to pursue a "relationship," as they say nowadays.

Most weeks, though, the preacher would take turns going to a parishioner's house for Sunday dinner, and it seemed that his visits to our house occurred more often than most. "How you doin', Reverend?" Granddaddy would ask, welcoming him. Reverend was privileged, as Mama would always make him her delicious chicken and dressing. It was the custom that we kids were not allowed to eat until the Reverend had finished his meal. He'd stay at the table, sitting with my aunts and uncles, talking about public and community affairs. Sometimes they'd have discussions about the Bible, politics, or the war. Reverend was long-winded and could talk forever.

My cousins and I would peek through the door and watch him devour the chicken. "Oh no, Reverend's got the drumstick!" Of course, my grandmother would say, "Reverend, come and have some more."

"Why, sister, I think I will have another piece," he'd reply, and we'd sigh in frustration. He'd eat until he was full and then sit back, patting his big stomach. He'd relax and talk some more until it was time for dessert, usually a three- or four-layer coconut cake. Finally, they would get up from the table, and we would rush the kitchen. We were starving! The Reverend would ask, "How you children doing?" and all we'd be thinking was "We don't have time to answer you, Reverend. We just want to get to the food!"

Martin Lawrence's Thyme Fried Chicken

He's one of the best at making me laugh—and he also makes a mean fried chicken! Make sure the oil is hot enough before you plunge the chicken pieces in, and you'll get a great-tasting result.

Serves 4

½ cup milk
1 chicken, cut into pieces
2 egg yolks
1 cup all-purpose flour

Hot oil for deep frying
1 tablespoon Creole seasoning
1 teaspoon dried thyme

Place the milk in a shallow bowl and add the chicken. Soak for 1 minute. Place the egg yolks in a shallow bowl and beat to mix. Place the flour in another shallow bowl. Heat about 2 inches of oil in a large, deep skillet over medium heat until hot.

Drain the chicken pieces and sprinkle with the Creole seasoning and thyme. Coat with egg yolk and dip in the flour. Fry in the hot oil until crispy and cooked through.

Isaac's Roasted Crispy Chick

Like a lot of people, I'm intrigued by the assortment of new cooking appliances that come on the market. Most of the time, I realize that I don't need what they're selling, that the item would just take up space on my counter. But I'm happy to sing the praises of a vertical roaster for baking chicken. It's healthier, because all the fat drips down to the pan in the bottom pan, and the chicken bastes itself.

Serves 2

1 3½–pound chicken
2 tablespoons soy sauce
1 teaspoon chopped fresh sage
⅛ teaspoon curry powder
⅛ teaspoon ground Jamaican allspice

⅛ teaspoon lemon pepper
Vertical roaster for a small chicken
½ cup water
Salt to taste
Pepper to taste

Preheat oven to 400 degrees.

With your fingertips, gently loosen the skin of the chicken from the breast and the back. Rub the meat under the skin with half the soy sauce and sprinkle with the sage, curry powder, allspice, and lemon pepper.

Set the chicken on the vertical roaster and place the roaster in a shallow baking pan. Pour the water in the bottom of the roasting pan and drizzle the chicken with the remaining soy sauce. Sprinkle the chicken with salt and pepper.

Roast the chicken until it is so crisp that you can eat the entire tip of the wing, if you have a taste for it: 35 to 40 minutes.

Serve with Candied "Ooooh Baby" Carrots (see page 50).

Mahogany Chicken Wings

Whenever I make these wings for friends, they always want to know how I get the skin such a fantastic rich shade of brown. It's all in the sauce, I tell them—and now I'm sharing my secret with you.

Serves 8 to 10

MARINADE
1 cup plus 2 tablespoons hoisin sauce
¾ cup plum sauce
½ cup light soy sauce
⅓ cup apple cider vinegar
¼ cup dry sherry

¼ cup honey
6 green onions, minced, greens included
6 large cloves garlic, minced

4 pounds chicken wings, tips removed,
*   separated at joint, if desired*

The day before serving: In a large bowl, combine the marinade ingredients and mix well. Add the chicken wings and toss to coat. Cover and refrigerate 24 hours.

The next day: Preheat oven to 375 degrees.

Let wings come to room temperature. Line 1 or 2 roasting pans with heavy-duty aluminum foil. Coat 1 or 2 wire racks with Pam nonstick cooking spray and place in baking pan(s).

Drain chicken and reserve marinade. Arrange wings on rack(s) and roast for 30 minutes. Drain liquid from pan(s). Baste wings with marinade, turn them and baste again. Roast until wings turn mahogany color, about 30 minutes.

The wings can be frozen after they are cooked. Pour the remaining marinade over wings and freeze. To serve at a later date, defrost to room temperature and heat prior to serving.

Oscar-Winning

Seafood-and-Crab Cakes

A&R Bar-Be-Que Ribs

John Singleton's White Fish
with Crabmeat Stuffing

North Memphis
Hoecakes

Delta Fried
Catfish with
24-Hour Coleslaw

Chicken Stroganoff

I think the word *luscious* was invented when someone first tasted stroganoff, a rich and creamy sauce with Russian origins and often prepared with beef. I decided to create a version that featured chicken instead. This can be a good buffet party choice because it reheats well in a chafing dish.

Serves 4 to 6

½ cup vegetable oil
1½ pounds boneless, skinless chicken breasts,
   cut into strips
2 tablespoons butter
1 large onion
½ pound fresh mushrooms, sliced
1 celery stalk, chopped
1 teaspoon salt

1 teaspoon paprika
1 teaspoon dry mustard
About ¾ cup chicken broth
1 tablespoon all-purpose flour
1 cup sour cream
1 tablespoon Worcestershire sauce
Cooked noodles or rice

In a large skillet, heat oil over medium heat until hot. Add chicken and sauté until lightly browned and cooked through, about 5 minutes. Remove the chicken to a bowl and set aside.

Drain the oil from the skillet into a measuring cup and set aside.

In the same skillet, over medium-high heat, melt the butter. Add the onion, mushrooms, celery, salt, paprika, and mustard. Cook, stirring constantly, until vegetables are tender—about 5 minutes.

To the drippings from the chicken, add enough broth to make ¾ cup. Add the flour and stir until blended. Gradually stir the liquid into the vegetable mixture in the skillet and cook, stirring constantly, until the sauce thickens. Add the sour cream and stir until mixture is smooth. Add the Worcestershire sauce and heat, stirring (do not let boil). Add the chicken to sauce and serve over noodles or rice.

Oven Baked Chicken with Garden Sauce

This is one of the recipes I created for myself when I began trying to eat in a healthier way. I knew that baking a chicken was better for me than frying it, and I discovered that I could make a great-tasting sauce out of fresh vegetables. I tried it a number of times with different combinations, and each one made the meal an occasion. *Serves 4*

1 4-pound roasting chicken, cut into parts
Salt and pepper to taste
Frozen mixed vegetables, or vegetables of your choice

1 teaspoon cornstarch, plus additional as needed
Pinch of saffron

Preheat oven to 375 degrees.

Season the chicken with salt and pepper. In a shallow roasting pan, bake for approximately 17 minutes a pound, until the pieces are lightly browned. In a saucepan, cook the vegetables according to package directions. While stirring constantly, add cornstarch until the liquid reaches the consistency of a smooth white sauce. Add the saffron, mixing very well to combine. Season with salt and pepper. Remove chicken from oven, pour the garden sauce over the chicken, and return to oven for approximately 15 minutes more.

Great over noodles or rice.

Josephina's Chicken Stir-Fry

In New York City (where I live now and do my radio show on KISS–FM), there are hundreds of restaurants to choose from. Josephina's, just across from Lincoln Center, has become one of my favorites. Everything on the menu tastes great and is good for your health. This recipe for the chicken stir-fry is full of flavor and has only 256 calories per serving.

Serves 4

*1½ pounds skinless, boneless chicken breasts,
    pounded thin*
1 tablespoon virgin olive oil
1 teaspoon finely chopped fresh gingerroot
1 teaspoon finely chopped garlic
1 cup broccoli florets
½ cup 1-inch pieces asparagus
½ cup thinly sliced bell pepper
½ cup thinly sliced carrots
⅓ cup low-sodium soy sauce

¼ cup water
1 tablespoon chili-garlic paste
1 teaspoon dark sesame oil
½ cup thinly sliced bok choy
½ cup thinly sliced shiitake mushrooms
½ cup fresh snow pea pods
Freshly ground black pepper to taste
3 tablespoons thinly sliced green onions
Cooked brown rice

Slice the chicken breasts into 3x½-inch strips.

Heat the olive oil in a nonstick wok or large skillet over medium-high heat; add the chicken and stir-fry 2 minutes. Add the ginger, garlic, broccoli, asparagus, bell pepper, and carrots and cook 3 minutes longer, stirring frequently.

Add the soy sauce, water, chili-garlic paste, sesame oil, bok choy, mushrooms, and snow peas. Continue to stir-fry until the carrots and asparagus are cooked through but still firm, about 2 minutes. Add the black pepper and green onions and stir. Serve over brown rice.

Steve Harvey's Stuffed Rolled Chicken Breast over Sweet Potato Risotto

Whether he's hosting *Showtime at the Apollo* or starring in his own television show, Steve Harvey knows how to command a crowd. The same is true when he's in charge of the kitchen, as you'll see when you serve this dish to company. I really like his version of risotto flavored with sweet potatoes, which makes a sophisticated dish taste like down-home.

Serves 4

4 boneless chicken breast halves
3 asparagus stalks, thinly sliced
1 carrot, cut into thin strips
1 onion, thinly sliced
1 stick butter
1 12-ounce box risotto

Salt to taste
About ½ cup chicken broth
1 sweet potato, peeled, boiled, and mashed
4 white mushrooms, finely chopped
½ cup heavy cream
Toothpicks

Place the chicken breasts between 2 sheets of plastic wrap and pound with a kitchen mallet until thin. Arrange the asparagus, carrot, and a few onion slices over the middle of each and roll up chicken to enclose the vegetables. Secure with toothpicks and set aside.

In a large ovenproof skillet, melt half the butter over medium-high heat and sauté the remaining onions until caramelized, about 10 minutes. Add the risotto and salt and cook, stirring, for 2 minutes. When the risotto is golden, stir in ½ cup chicken broth. Reduce the heat to low and add the mashed sweet potato. Mix well, adding a little chicken broth, if necessary, to soften the sweet potato. Simmer, stirring occasionally, until risotto is tender, about 45 minutes.

While the risotto cooks, in another skillet, over medium heat, melt the remaining half of the butter. Add the chicken rolls. Cook, turning the rolls, until they are lightly browned on all sides and cooked through, about 10 minutes.

Preheat oven to 275 degrees. When the risotto mixture is done, place chicken rolls on top of the risotto and bake for 5 to 10 minutes.

While the chicken bakes, add the mushrooms to the drippings in the skillet used to brown the chicken and sauté over medium-high heat until browned. Add the heavy cream and heat to boiling, stirring to loosen any browned bits from bottom of pan. Season the mushroom sauce with salt and serve with the chicken and risotto.

"Gonna Get Some" Cornish Game Hens with Wild Rice Stuffing

This is the dinner I like to cook for someone special, when I hope that after dinner ends, the evening is just beginning! Along with this I like to serve green peas with pearl onions and carrots with a maple syrup glaze on the side. (Why do I make four hens when I'm expecting just one guest? Well, you never know how big an appetite you and your guest will have!)

Serves 4

4 Rock Cornish game hens
2 tablespoons chopped fresh sage
1⅛ teaspoons curry powder
1 teaspoon ground allspice
1 teaspoon lemon pepper
Salt to taste
Freshly ground black pepper to taste
2 tablespoons soy sauce
4½ cups water
1½ cups wild rice, rinsed in several changes of water
½ cup raisins

1 tablespoon tarragon
1 teaspoon Chinese five-spice powder
1 teaspoon chopped fresh basil
1 teaspoon celery seed
½ cup pineapple chunks
1 teaspoon butter
1 11-ounce can mandarin oranges with syrup
¼ cup maple syrup
1 teaspoon grated orange zest
¼ teaspoon grated nutmeg
¼ teaspoon cinnamon

Preheat oven to 350 degrees. Wash and dry the hens.

In a small bowl, combine 1 tablespoon sage, ⅛ teaspoon curry powder, allspice, lemon pepper, salt, and pepper. Gently pull the skin away from the breast of each hen, being careful not to tear the skin. Rub the spice mixture under the skin. Gently replace the skin. Rub the soy sauce over the hens.

Place the hens in a roasting pan just large enough to hold them. Add ½ cup water to the pan. Cover and roast for 30 to 45 minutes.

In a medium saucepan, heat 4 cups water to boiling. Add the wild rice and raisins. Stir in the remaining 1 tablespoon sage, the remaining 1 teaspoon curry powder, tarragon, five-spice powder, basil, and celery seed. Cook for 45 minutes. Just before the rice is done, add the pineapple and butter. Cover and set aside.

In another saucepan, combine the mandarin oranges with syrup, maple syrup, orange zest, nutmeg, and cinnamon. Heat slowly to boiling. Add 1 tablespoon of the sauce to the cooked rice. Set aside.

When the hens are done, stuff them with the rice mixture and return them to the pan. Brush with some of the orange sauce and bake until the glaze browns.

Serve with the remaining orange sauce on the side.

Wesley Snipes's Rum-Glazed Cornish Hens Stuffed with Apple-Sourdough Stuffing

Ever since I started doing the cooking, I've liked serving these small hens at an intimate dinner for two. When Wesley suggested his favorite recipe, I realized that he also shared my ideas about culinary seduction.

Serves 2

2 Rock Cornish game hens
2 tablespoons dark rum
Creole seasoning to taste
2 tablespoons olive oil
2 Granny Smith apples, chopped
1 large onion, chopped
1 clove garlic, minced

2 slices sourdough bread, crumbled
1 tablespoon white wine
1 sprig fresh thyme leaves, separated from stem
½ teaspoon freshly ground black pepper
½ teaspoon sea salt

Wash and dry hens and place in a roasting pan. Rub each with 1 tablespoon rum and sprinkle with Creole seasoning. Refrigerate for 1 hour.

Preheat oven to 325 degrees. In a medium skillet, heat olive oil over medium-high heat. Add the apples, onion, and garlic and sauté until the apples and onion are tender, about 10 minutes. Add the bread, wine, thyme, pepper, and salt and mix well. Remove pan from heat.

Stuff the Cornish hens with the bread mixture and place in the roasting pan. Cover with foil.

Bake hens for 1 hour, uncovering them for the last 15 minutes. The hens should be nice and brown.

Crispy Chicken Livers

Chicken livers are best cooked in an electric deep-fryer. These make a hearty breakfast or lunch.

Serves 2 to 4

1 pound chicken livers
1 cup vegetable oil
4 eggs
1 cup all-purpose flour

Salt to taste
Pepper to taste
Garlic powder to taste
1 cup Italian-style bread crumbs

Clean chicken livers and pat dry with paper towels. Heat the oil in an electric deep-fryer or a large, deep skillet over medium heat.

In a small bowl, beat the eggs. In a paper bag, combine the flour, salt, pepper, and garlic powder and shake to mix.

Dip chicken livers in eggs and place the livers in paper bag with the seasoned flour. Shake bag well to coat the livers. Shake off the excess flour. On a plate, roll the floured livers in Italian bread crumbs. Fry livers until browned and crispy.

Mushroom Cream Sauce

This is RFR—Recommended For Romancing the woman (or man) of your choice. This sauce, which I've ladled over chicken and pork, both looks and smells rich and delicious. Just be sure you're ready for the reaction you'll get! ***Makes about 2 cups***

2 tablespoons unsalted butter
½ pound small white mushrooms, cleaned
    and trimmed
1 small shallot, minced
6 sprigs fresh thyme, tied together with
    cotton string
¼ cup Chardonnay

¼ cup Myers rum or Cognac
1½ cups heavy cream
4 tablespoons unsalted butter, cut into
    ¼-inch cubes
Salt to taste
Freshly ground black pepper to taste

Heat a large skillet over medium heat, add the butter, and, when melted, sauté the mushrooms, shallot, and thyme until mushrooms are softened—4 to 5 minutes. Add the wine and rum and heat to boiling. Remove the mushrooms with a slotted spoon to a bowl and set aside. Boil the liquid in the skillet until about 3 tablespoons remain.

Add the cream to the liquid in the skillet, heat to simmering, and cook until reduced by half. Return the mushrooms to the cream and simmer until the sauce is the desired thickness.

Add the butter, bit by bit, to the sauce, stirring continually over medium heat without boiling the sauce. Remove the pan from the heat when all the butter has been added and the sauce is smooth, thick, and creamy. Discard the thyme.

Turkey
Never Had It
So Good

Heart & Soul Heart & Soul Heart & Soul Heart & Soul Heart & Soul Heart & Soul

Covington's Sunday Dinner Roasted Turkey with Cornbread Dressing and Giblet Gravy

No matter where I am in the world, this is the meal that takes me back home. It takes some time to do it right, especially for the cornbread dressing and giblet gravy, but it's truly worth it when you and your family finally taste this labor of love.   *Serves 10 to 12*

1 16-pound turkey, with giblets and neck
2 tablespoons unsalted butter, softened
Salt to taste
Pepper to taste
1 medium onion, peeled and cut into chunks
1 boiling potato, peeled and cut into chunks
1 large carrot, peeled and cut into chunks

GIBLET GRAVY
Giblets from the turkey plus 3 extra giblets
Neck bones from the turkey plus 3 extra
   turkey neck bones
¼ cup all-purpose flour
1 teaspoon dried sage
½ teaspoon dried sweet basil
½ teaspoon Chinese five-spice powder
2 tablespoons Mazola corn oil
1 onion, finely chopped
¼ cup chopped mushrooms
¾ cup evaporated milk
Salt to taste
Pepper to taste

CORNBREAD DRESSING
2 sticks unsalted butter
3 celery stalks, finely chopped
1½ red bell peppers, seeded and finely
   chopped
1½ green bell peppers, seeded and finely
   chopped
1 medium onion, finely chopped
3 bunches scallions, trimmed, green and
   white parts finely chopped
6 boxes Jiffy cornbread mix, baked according
   to package directions and cooled
1 tablespoon celery seed
1½ teaspoons dried sage
1½ teaspoons poultry seasoning
1½ teaspoons garlic powder
1½ teaspoons minced fresh cilantro
1½ teaspoons dried basil
1½ teaspoons Chinese five-spice powder
1½ teaspoons lemon pepper
½ teaspoon ground allspice
½ teaspoon curry powder
Sea salt to taste
Freshly ground black pepper to taste

For the turkey: Preheat oven to 350 degrees. Rinse the turkey inside and out with cold water and pat dry with paper towels. Using your hands, rub the turkey skin all over with the softened butter and then with salt and pepper. Place the turkey in a large roasting pan and fill the cavity with onion, potato, and carrot. Roast, basting occasionally with pan juices, until the thigh juices run clear when pricked with a fork, 3½ to 4 hours (20 minutes a pound). If the skin browns too quickly, loosely cover the turkey with foil for the remaining cooking time.

For the gravy: Put giblets and turkey necks in a large pot of water; cover and heat to boiling. Remove from heat and set aside to cool. Remove giblets and necks to a large bowl. Reserve giblet water. Chop giblets; remove meat from neck bone and crumble with your hands. Separate one-fourth of the chopped giblets and neck meat for the gravy and reserve the remainder for the dressing.

In a small bowl, combine flour with sage, basil, and five-spice powder and mix well. Heat the oil in a medium saucepan over medium-high heat and sauté the onion and mushrooms until brown and caramelized, about 10 minutes. Add 1 cup of reserved giblet water and the seasoned flour. Stir until mixture is smooth and begins to bubble. Add the evaporated milk, stirring constantly until the gravy thickens. Add enough of the giblet water to make gravy the desired consistency. Stir in reserved giblets and season with salt and pepper. Turn off the heat, cover, and set aside until turkey is served. Reheat the gravy before serving.

For the cornbread dressing: In a large skillet, melt 1 stick of butter over medium-high heat. Add the celery, bell peppers, onion, and scallions and sauté until vegetables are softened, about 10 minutes. Crumble the cornbread into a large mixing bowl, add the vegetable mixture and the melted butter in the pan, celery seed, sage, poultry seasoning, garlic powder, cilantro, basil, five-spice powder, lemon pepper, allspice, and curry powder. Add reserved giblets and neck meat to the cornbread mixture and mix gently but thoroughly. Slowly ladle giblet water into the cornbread mixture, mixing as you add, and use only enough liquid to moisten to the desired consistency. Season with salt and pepper. Melt the remaining stick of butter and drizzle into the dressing. Stir gently and taste as you add the butter—you may not need the whole stick.

Half an hour before the turkey is done, remove it from the oven and set aside. Remove the vegetables. Place the dressing in the cavity of the turkey, spreading the extra dressing around the turkey, and return the roasting pan to the oven for an additional 45 minutes. (If you have leftover dressing, fill an ovenproof dish and place in oven with the turkey for 10 to 15 minutes. You want it to have a beautiful crust.)

Serve with Wendy's Fresh Cranberry Salad (see page 154).

Deep-Fried Jive Turkey

This is a wonderful southern recipe that has become a Thanksgiving tradition in many homes. But frying a whole turkey is an activity in which you definitely have to take great care. Wear the longest protective gloves you've got, and use extra-long tongs or a stick to lower the turkey into the pot, because it's likely to bubble and splatter (and nothing burns like hot oil).

Serves 10 to 12

2 tablespoons Creole seasoning, or to taste
2 teaspoons dried thyme
2 teaspoons dried sage leaves
2 teaspoons dried oregano
2 teaspoons dried basil leaves

2 cloves garlic, minced
1 10- to 12-pound turkey
5 gallons peanut oil
Liquid marinade (optional)

Grind and mix seasonings together. Rub mixture over turkey, adding a little more Creole seasoning to your taste. Fold the wings on top of the turkey to secure, or clip them. Marinate turkey overnight (if using liquid marinade, inject it under the skin before letting it sit overnight).

In a 10-gallon pot, heat 5 gallons of peanut oil to 360 degrees. Fry turkey until the juices run clear when pierced with a fork, about 45 minutes, or 3 minutes for every pound.

Let turkey sit for 15 to 20 minutes before carving.

Cooking for My Kids

When my kids were teenagers, I found myself cooking a lot more than I ever expected to. At one time, five of them came to live with me in Memphis. Suddenly, I was Mr. Mom. I needed to get organized to keep the household going, and so I set up a bulletin board and posted the kids' weekly chores, along with the menus for each day of the week. I wasn't as strict as Mama had been with me, but I still made them do their chores.

When they complained about pitching in, I'd remind them about what life had been like for me growing up in the country. They were shocked when I described how I used to work in the fields, picking and chopping cotton alongside the adults.

"You chopped cotton?" they asked in disbelief. For them, it was like hearing a tale from the Dark Ages—the idea of me working as a field hand doing hard, manual labor. The life I'd lived back then, a life that had seemed so ordinary to me, was downright foreign to them. They had no idea what a struggle it had been for me to get an education, what it took for me to decide to go back to school and finish up. It was important to me that my kids understand what it took for me to get where I was. Even if they were living a more privileged life than I had, I still wanted them to develop a good work ethic.

I decided the best lesson I could teach my kids was to take responsibility for themselves. When they got home from school, they had to make time for two kinds of homework: their school assignments *and* their chores. I gave each of them an allowance, but if they flunked a test in school or failed to do their work around the house, I had no hesitation about hitting them where it hurt—in their wallets. I'd simply say, "You've got to take some responsibility!" That was the rule in my household.

Maybe they didn't like doing all their chores, but they seemed to enjoy the time spent helping me in the kitchen, mostly chopping vegetables or cleaning up. They loved my food so much, on more than one occasion it made their mothers jealous that our kids preferred my cooking to theirs! I would cook breakfast in the morning and get them off to school. Later, I'd pick them up from school and start making dinner. Feeding and raising those kids totally dominated my life in those years, which gave me enormous respect for the moms—and dads—who hold down jobs and hold their families together.

I cooked all kinds of meals for my kids, who liked just about everything I served them. They especially liked ribs, of course, served with all their favorite fixings. And while I was often on the road during Thanksgiving, I made a point of getting the family together for a turkey dinner over the Christmas holidays whenever I could.

With my family in Memphis, late 1970s. From left, top: my son Vincent, daughter Veronica, nieces Ida Rankin, Bonita Young, and Valerie Brooks, and daughter Felicia; bottom: me, my daughter Heather, grandmother Rushia Wade, daughter Melanie, sister Willette Rankin, and daughter Nikki.

Cheesy Turkey Tetrazzini

This classic, 1950s-style dish has always been considered a great way to use up leftover turkey, but once I started eating more poultry and less red meat, I stopped waiting for leftovers and stirred this up much more often. You can substitute chicken or tuna for the turkey, and still get a tasty result. (I gave up drinking alcohol more than thirty years ago, but I still cook with spirits—like dry sherry—from time to time. The alcohol burns off in the cooking, and all that's left is some great flavor.)   *Serves 6 to 8*

8 ounces spaghetti	*¼ cup all-purpose flour*
1½ pounds cooked turkey, diced	*2 cups milk*
2 tablespoons chopped pimientos	*1 cup chicken broth*
½ teaspoon chopped fresh parsley	*¼ cup dry sherry*
4 tablespoons butter	*Dash of salt*
½ cup finely chopped onion	*Dash of ground white pepper*
¼ cup sliced mushrooms	*8 ounces sharp cheddar cheese, shredded*

Preheat oven to 350 degrees. Grease a 3-quart baking dish.

Cook spaghetti according to package directions. Drain and place in a large bowl. Add the turkey, pimientos, and parsley.

In a medium skillet, melt the butter over medium heat and sauté the onion and mushrooms until softened, about 5 minutes. Blend in the flour and gradually add the milk, chicken broth, and sherry, stirring constantly. Heat to boiling, stirring, over medium-low heat. Simmer until thickened and season with salt and pepper. Add the sauce to the spaghetti mixture and toss to coat. Spread the mixture into the prepared baking dish and sprinkle cheese over top.

Bake until heated through and cheese is bubbly, 35 to 40 minutes.

Ike's "Three Tough Guys"
Turkey Meat Loaf

Not long after I hit the top of the charts with *Hot Buttered Soul* and *Shaft,* my agent got a call about a movie project for me. This time, they wanted Isaac Hayes, the actor. The year was 1972, and Dino De Laurentiis was producing a movie called *Three Tough Guys,* with Fred Williamson and Lino Ventura. Since I'd succeeded in filling theaters with my concerts, the movie people figured I might be an audience draw in their picture. I hoped they were right, because I wanted the chance to act, and so I took the job.

Serves 4 to 6

SAUCE
1 cup ketchup
½ cup frozen apple juice concentrate, thawed
¼ cup apple cider vinegar
1 tablespoon brown sugar
1 tablespoon tomato paste
1 tablespoon soy sauce
1 teaspoon sea salt
1 teaspoon garlic powder

MEAT LOAF
2 pounds ground turkey
1 tablespoon minced fresh basil or 1 teaspoon
    dried
1 tablespoon minced fresh cilantro
    or 1 teaspoon dried
1 tablespoon minced fresh sage or 1 teaspoon
    dried
1 tablespoon minced fresh tarragon
    or 1 teaspoon dried

¼ teaspoon Chinese five-spice powder
¼ teaspoon ground Jamaican allspice
¼ teaspoon Old Bay seasoning
⅛ teaspoon curry powder
1 egg, beaten
2 tablespoons dry sherry
2 tablespoons barbecue sauce
1 tablespoon soy sauce
1 tablespoon apple cider vinegar
½ cup chopped green bell pepper
½ cup chopped red bell pepper
½ cup chopped yellow bell pepper
½ cup chopped yellow or spring onions
½ cup chopped celery
½ cup sliced fresh mushrooms
1 clove garlic, minced
About ½ cup Italian-style bread crumbs
About ½ cup Ritz cracker crumbs

Preheat oven to 350 degrees.

For the sauce: In a medium saucepan, combine the ketchup, apple juice concentrate, vinegar, brown sugar, tomato paste, soy sauce, and salt and mix well. Heat to boiling and stir in the garlic powder. Over low heat, simmer the sauce, stirring occasionally, until it is the consistency of ketchup.

Here, in my film debut as actor in **Three Tough Guys,** *I take aim at the Chicago waterfront.*

For the meat loaf: Place the turkey in a large bowl and, working with your hands, knead the turkey to separate it. Add the basil, cilantro, sage, tarragon, five-spice powder, allspice, Old Bay seasoning, and curry powder and mix lightly to work them into the turkey. Add the egg and lightly knead into the meat. Add the sherry, barbecue sauce, soy sauce, and vinegar and knead in. Mix in vegetables and garlic.

Knead in just enough (equal amounts of) bread crumbs and Ritz cracker crumbs until the consistency of the turkey mixture is just firm enough to form into a loaf.

Roll the loaf in the remaining Ritz cracker crumbs and place it in a roasting pan. Pour half of the sauce on top of the loaf. Cover with the pan lid and bake until the end of the meat loaf registers 160 degrees on an instant-read thermometer, 60 to 75 minutes. Remove the lid, and let the turkey loaf brown for an additional 10 minutes.

Serve with the remaining sauce and Smashing Mashed Potatoes (see page 45).

Baked Vidalia Onions with Italian Turkey Stuffing

There's something kind of spectacular about serving a huge Vidalia onion, stuffed to the brim, as a dinner entrée. If you've never tried this southern-style delicacy, give it a try when you spot these sweet onions in your market. Presented this way, it's a meal in itself.

Serves 4

4 large Vidalia onions, peeled
¾ pound Italian turkey sausage, removed from casing
½ cup sliced mushrooms
4 ounces herb stuffing mix

⅛ teaspoon thyme
⅛ teaspoon oregano
About 4 tablespoons cream cheese
½ cup grated Parmesan cheese

Preheat oven to 350 degrees. Grease a baking dish just large enough to hold the onions.

Trim the onions on the bottom so they sit flat. Remove and chop the centers, leaving several layers of outer rings.

In a large skillet over medium-high heat, combine the onion centers with the sausage and mushrooms and sauté, breaking up the sausage with a spoon, until the onion is tender, about 10 minutes. Remove pan from the heat and add the stuffing, thyme, oregano, and just enough cream cheese to moisten.

Spoon the stuffing into the onions, heaping about ½ inch above the top. Place filled onions in the prepared dish. Bake until onions are tender, about 25 minutes.

Sprinkle onions with the Parmesan cheese and bake 5 minutes longer. Serve hot.

Meals That Bring Me Home

When you're away from home all the time, you tend to hunger for the foods that take you back there, if only for as long as dinner lasts. In the early 1980s, I lived in London for about a year. It was a great city in a lot of ways, but getting used to the food over there took some doing. When Mark, a fellow American expatriate, and I got talking one day about Thanksgiving, and about all the familiar dishes that made the meal so hard to miss, Mark offered to host a Thanksgiving dinner at his flat. We decided to invite all our English friends from the health club where we both worked out.

The challenge to making an authentic southern American Thanksgiving dinner was finding the ingredients. We found most of what we needed, but the local markets didn't have everything I wanted. Luckily, a girlfriend of mine flew over from the United States with six boxes of Jiffy cornbread mix so I could make my traditional stuffing. When we served dinner, our British friends cheered all the American specialties, but they especially loved my cornbread dressing. When they told me, "Oh, Isaac, this is so good!" they weren't just being polite, either—they kept coming back for more! In the middle of the meal I stood up and offered a toast: "We took our independence from you, for which we're truly thankful. Now it's our pleasure to give a little something back. Let's celebrate!" Thousands of miles from home, we had a wonderful time sharing the foods that make every Thanksgiving a day to remember.

Strokin', Smokin' Turkey Legs

The combination of the smoked turkey with great barbecue sauce is a real winner. Maybe you've never thought about preparing turkey this way, but you'll be astonished at how much difference a couple of hours in the pit will make! *Serves 6*

6 turkey legs
Salt to taste
Barbecue sauce of your choice

Wash the turkey legs and pat dry with paper towels. Sprinkle with salt.

Place legs in a smoker or an open barbecue pit, making sure the legs are not touching.

Cook turkey legs until tender, turning every 30 to 40 minutes, for about 2 hours. The internal temperature of the turkey should not be less than 180 degrees.

Remove the legs from the smoker and "stroke" with barbecue sauce.

Cook until the juices are sealed in, 15 to 20 minutes, and serve.

■ CHEF'S NOTE: You can use any kind of commercial or homemade barbecue sauce. Or try my Memphis Magic Sauces (see the back of the book).

Terri Vaughn's Turdunken

Talk about a dish that says Wow! Turdunken usually calls for a turkey stuffed with a duck and a chicken, but this version beloved by the beautiful and talented costar of *The Steve Harvey Show* substitutes crawfish for the chicken. This recipe is ambitious but not as hard to fix as it sounds. Your butcher can debone your turkey or duck. Add my special Tropical Glaze for extra pizzazz.

Serves 8 to 10

4 tablespoons butter	4 sprigs parsley, chopped
2 onions, chopped	2 sprigs thyme
2 shallots, minced	1 teaspoon sea salt
2 pounds cleaned crawfish	1 teaspoon pepper
2 red bell peppers, chopped	3 cups steamed rice
8 mushrooms, chopped	1 10-pound turkey, boned
4 tablespoons Creole seasoning	1 5-pound duck, boned

Preheat oven to 325 degrees. In a large skillet, melt the butter over medium heat. Add the onions and shallots and sauté until caramelized, about 15 minutes. Add the crawfish, bell pepper, mushrooms, 3 tablespoons Creole seasoning, parsley, thyme, salt, and pepper and sauté until crawfish are cooked and red peppers are tender, about 5 minutes. Transfer the crawfish mixture to a large bowl; add the rice and mix with a large fork to combine.

Wash the turkey and duck and pat dry with paper towels. Stuff the cavity of the turkey with the crawfish stuffing, leaving enough room for the duck to fit inside turkey cavity. After placing duck inside turkey, stuff duck with reminder of stuffing. Tie the cavity of the turdunken with string so the stuffing will remain in place.

Place the turdunken in a large roasting pan and sprinkle with 1 tablespoon of Creole seasoning. Cover with foil and cook through, about 4½ hours, uncovering the last 30 minutes to brown the turdunken.

HEALTHY COOKING, HEALTHY LIVING

I didn't start out with any idea of what it meant to live and eat in a healthy way. I started smoking when I was twelve years old; lots of the kids in my school did. Alcohol and tobacco were a part of my life until well into my twenties. Then I quit, cold turkey, both smoking and drinking, in 1967.

I was in Atlanta at the time at a DJ convention, and I was run-down and carousing around the clock. I felt like I was going to die that night, but I guess I was just having an anxiety attack. Still, it was enough to convince me to change the way I was living. Right then and there, I just quit—and I haven't touched a drop of liquor or smoked a cigarette since.

It was also about that time that I first got interested in the subject of healthy eating and healthy cooking. Some musician friends who belonged to the Nation of Islam had told me about the dietary guidelines they follow as part of their religion. The most significant one required that they abstain from eating pork, a food I'd enjoyed since childhood. But a lot of what they said made sense to me, and so for a long time, I stopped eating pork.

A few years later, I was spending some time in Los Angeles and started learning more about health foods. In the early seventies, the hippies were eating nuts and grains and raisins, talking about how good they felt. I figured, okay, I'll give it a try.

I started reading books on the subject and visiting health food stores to see what was available. I became really intrigued by the possibility of living and eating in a healthy way—not dying prematurely of a heart attack or stroke, which had been a way of life in my old neighborhood.

When I started hearing that eating health foods could make a real difference, when I learned that by eating better, you could avoid developing these illnesses, I knew that was what I wanted to do.

I bought my first juicer because everyone was saying you needed one if you wanted to be really healthy. (I must have given away twenty-five or thirty of those things over the years as gifts!) I started juicing carrots and apples, then other vegetables too. I read the book *Back to Eden* by Jethro Kloss, and it reinforced what I'd been hearing. I started learning about teas, and then about macrobiotics. I became very focused on understanding how to eat in these new, healthy ways, but it was a lot of work.

Here I am (center) with the Crusaders basketball team, New York, 1998.

Cooking and eating health foods back in those days was a real challenge because the food was so bland—it tasted like nothing. You had to be totally dedicated to it. I realized then that if I was going to keep eating this way, I'd have to learn to get some real taste into the foods I prepared.

Over the years, I've tried a lot of different ways of eating. For a while I went totally vegetarian; another time, I went on regular fruit fasts, and for a time I stopped eating breads. Then I backed off dairy for a while. I was constantly experimenting. Even though I'm the kind of person who can eat the same thing for days on end and not get bored, I was determined to find ways to vary the routine. What really kept me focused was deciding that now I was going to eat to live, not live to eat.

It made sense to me: If you live to eat, you're likely to eat everything in sight, but if you eat just to live, you're going to eat only the right things, the foods that help you live a healthy life.

What's Good for the Heart and Soul: Salads and Pasta

Heart & Soul Heart & Soul Heart & Soul Heart & Soul Heart & Soul Heart & Soul

Chilled Collard Green Salad

This recipe shows you how to use what chefs call an ice bath to speedily halt the cooking process once you've cooked your vegetables to exactly the right tenderness. This way of preparing collard greens takes a little more time than serving them raw, but the flavor makes it well worth the trouble. *Serves 2 to 4*

⅓ cup olive oil
1 bunch collard greens, washed, tough stems
    and veins removed, and leaves chopped
½ onion, chopped
3 strips bacon, cooked and crumbled
1 hard-boiled egg, peeled and thinly sliced

1 tablespoon sour cream
Pinch of sea salt
1 tomato, sliced
2 roasted cloves garlic
2 ounces smoked turkey, slivered

In a large skillet, heat the oil over medium-high heat until hot. Add the chopped greens and onion and sauté until greens are wilted, about 2 minutes.

Transfer the greens to a bowl of ice water to shock the greens to keep their color. Drain the greens, dry, and place in a large bowl. Add the bacon, egg, sour cream, and salt and toss to coat. Cover and refrigerate until chilled.

Serve garnished with sliced tomatoes, roasted garlic, and smoked turkey.

24-Hour Coleslaw

Don't let the name of this recipe discourage you from trying it. Just as many baked goods are better the day after they're made, so too are some spirited salads! I've traveled from end to end of this country, and I've eaten all kinds of coleslaw along the way. This version takes a little more patience than some others I've made, but I think the extra effort is definitely worth it. Serve this on top of Lu's Chopped BBQ Pork sandwich (see page 73) or with catfish.

Serves 6 to 8

1 medium red or green cabbage, shredded
1 large carrot, shredded
4 green onions, thinly sliced
2 medium-size tart apples, chopped
½ cup sugar

1 cup apple cider vinegar
1 teaspoon celery seed
1 teaspoon salt
1 teaspoon prepared mustard
½ cup vegetable oil

In a large bowl, combine the cabbage, carrot, green onions, and apples. Pour the sugar over the mixture and mix thoroughly.

In a small bowl, combine the vinegar, celery seed, salt, and mustard and mix well. Gradually whisk in the oil until the dressing is blended and smooth and pour over the cabbage mixture. Toss until well coated. Cover and refrigerate for 24 hours, stirring at least once to mix.

Strokin', Smokin' Turkey Legs

"Gonna Get Some" Cornish Game Hens

with Wild Rice Stuffing

Isaac's Healthy Mixed-Green Salad

Zesti-Luv Lemon
Meringue Pie

Pearlie's Triple
Chocolate Trifle

Bubba Lee's Potato Salad

I've been eating potato salad ever since Mama switched me from baby food to the real thing! Potatoes are cheap and filling, and when you add a little bit of this and that, you end up with a dish good enough for a family reunion—or anytime at all. Some people like to use red-skinned potatoes and leave the skins on, but I was raised on skinless potato salad, and that's what I like best.

Serves 4 to 6

2 pounds potatoes (about 6 medium)
¼ cup finely chopped green bell pepper
¼ cup finely chopped onion
¼ cup finely chopped celery
1 teaspoon salt
⅛ teaspoon ground white pepper
¼ cup white vinegar
2 tablespoons sweet relish

2 tablespoons chopped pimientos
2 tablespoons sliced olives, jalapeños, or capers
½ cup mayonnaise
Dash of prepared mustard (mainly for color)
3 hard-boiled eggs for garnish
2 tablespoons chopped fresh parsley
Dash of paprika

Cook the potatoes in steamer or boil until soft, about 30 minutes. (Steaming the potatoes will help preserve the nutrients.)

Cool and peel the potatoes and cut into cubes. Place in a large bowl and add the green pepper, onion, celery, salt, pepper, vinegar, relish, pimientos, and olives. Mix gently but thoroughly. Cover and refrigerate for at least 6 hours before serving.

Immediately before serving, add mayonnaise and toss until mixture is well coated. Garnish with eggs and parsley and sprinkle with paprika.

Spinach Salad with Poppy Seed Dressing

This is the kind of hearty salad that can easily convince you that you're having a meal. A traditional spinach salad may not include ingredients like the oranges and cheese, but they add a tremendous amount of flavor and color to the dish. *Serves 4 to 6*

SALAD
- ½ pound fresh baby spinach, washed well and dried
- ¼ cup thinly sliced mushrooms
- 8 strips turkey bacon, cooked until crisp and crumbled
- 1 medium red onion, thinly sliced
- 1 11-ounce can mandarin orange segments, drained
- ¼ pound blue cheese, crumbled

POPPY SEED DRESSING
- ⅓ cup red wine
- ⅓ cup vinegar
- ⅓ cup vegetable oil
- ¼ cup honey
- 4 teaspoons poppy seeds
- 4 teaspoons minced onions
- ¾ teaspoon ground mace

For the salad: In a large bowl, combine the spinach, mushrooms, bacon, onion, orange segments, and blue cheese and toss to mix.

For the dressing: In a small bowl, combine the wine, vinegar, oil, honey, poppy seeds, onion, and mace and whisk until blended and smooth. Pour over the spinach salad and toss to coat. Serve immediately.

Isaac's Healthy Mixed-Green Salad

I've eaten this salad in so many variations, I'm not giving you any specific proportions. This recipe can be adjusted to fit your mood, your taste, your budget, and whatever is in your refrigerator. If your goal is getting more servings a day of healthy vegetables, this is a great way to start.

Serves 4 to 6

*20 ounces mixed salad greens, mesclun, or
 your favorite grocery store mix*
1 carrot, shredded
10 grape tomatoes
1 hothouse cucumber, thinly sliced

*1 cup bite-size pieces of fried chicken, fish,
 grilled chicken, or shrimp*
*Oil and vinegar or your favorite salad
 dressing*

In a large bowl, combine the salad greens, carrot, tomatoes, cucumbers, and fish, chicken, or shrimp. Toss to mix.

Dress with oil and vinegar or your favorite dressing and serve.

Rabbit Food

My philosophy is: Eat healthy foods but also allow yourself a few indulgences. Sometimes you have to reward yourself with some decadent stuff, but only every now and again.

I've developed a taste for what are called raw, live foods, and I still juice a lot. Guys tease me for eating all that rabbit food, and I tell them to put a steak in the ground and cover it up. Come back in two or three days and see what happens. It'll be so rotten you can smell it even before you uncover it.

But put some bean sprouts in the ground and cover them up and come back

At the photo shoot for the jacket of this book, New York, 2000.

later. In three or four days, they'll be sprouting, because they're alive. Any food at the sprouting stage is at its richest nutritionally because it's still actively growing. Life begets life. Sometimes, though, I'm eating so clean and healthy that if I ate a candy bar, I'd get the sniffles. My body gets so it can't tolerate anything that isn't good for it.

Occasionally, I go on a binge, eating old favorite foods, and then I'll fast and cleanse myself, and come out feeling great. I remember how my radio audience became concerned about one of my fasts, they kept calling in, worried as I was counting down the days. But I feel much better after I fast. That's why people look at me and say, "Wow, man, you look like you did on the album cover back in 1973." And the guys who tease me about eating rabbit food? I just tell them, "Rabbits multiply."

Vegetable Salad

The secret to making a fresh vegetable salad appealing is mixing up colors and textures that please the eye *and* the taste buds. Keep as many different fresh vegetables on hand as you can make room for, so you'll be ready to chop up a festive blend at a moment's notice.

Serves 4 to 6

1 small bunch broccoli, cut into bite-size
  florets and stalks sliced
1 small head cauliflower, cut into bite-size
  florets
1 small zucchini, sliced paper-thin
2 large carrots, scraped and sliced paper-thin

¼ pound mushrooms, thinly sliced
1 small red or green bell pepper, seeded and
  cut into matchsticks

Oil and vinegar or your favorite salad
  dressing to taste

In a pretty glass bowl, combine all ingredients. Mix with oil and vinegar or your favorite salad dressing and serve immediately.

Tropical Fruit Salad with Plain Yogurt Dressing

I f you're looking to eat something light before a workout, this melange of fresh fruit will provide you with energy to burn. Vary the fruits in it according to what looks good at the green market, and buy organic when you can get it.

Serves 6 to 8

3 bananas, peeled and sliced
1 11-ounce can mandarin orange segments, drained
1 cup strawberries, halved
½ cup green seedless grapes
½ cup red seedless grapes
2 kiwis, peeled, thinly sliced

½ cup raisins
½ cup chopped nuts
¼ cup shredded coconut
1 15¼-ounce can fruit cocktail, drained
1 pint plain yogurt
Your favorite sweetener to taste

In a large clear bowl, combine the fruits, nuts, and coconut and mix well. Cover and refrigerate at least 2 hours.

Serve fruit in small bowls and top with plain yogurt just before eating.

Sweeten individually with your favorite sweetener.

Rome's Summer Watergate Salad

Here's a great summer dessert that, according to Rome Douglas, is "tasty, cool, and fun for me to make for a crowd!" Pearlie is Rome's aunt, and Rome, who *loves* to eat, asked to make the desserts when I came for a visit and a wonderful meal. You can use as much lime Jell-O as you like in this recipe. Sometimes I make it very light, using just one package; other times, I may decide I want a much stronger flavor and add most of a second package.   *Serves 6 to 8*

1 12-ounce container Cool Whip
1 3-ounce box lime Jell-O, prepared
    according to package directions and
    chilled until firm

1 8-ounce can crushed pineapple, drained
1 cup chopped pecans
Maraschino cherries with stems

Empty Cool Whip into a large bowl and add Jell-O, drained crushed pineapple, and chopped pecans and mix well. Spoon into wineglasses or your favorite dessert bowls and top with maraschino cherries.

Wendy's Fresh Cranberry Salad

Wendy is Pearlie's daughter and my goddaughter. She has always known me as "Bubba" and has been a part of my life since she was born in 1971, at a really high point in my career. Wendy has been health conscious all her life, especially when she was working as a model, and she shares my commitment to staying physically fit and taking vitamins. Encouraged by her mother to prepare healthy, nutritious meals, she likes to create all kinds of salads for us to enjoy together. This sweet and colorful recipe is a holiday must! Nobody needs to know just how much vitamin C those fresh berries provide. They'll be too busy enjoying the creamy, crunchy flavors in each and every bite.   *Serves 4 to 6*

2 cups chopped fresh cranberries
2 Golden Delicious apples, peeled and
    chopped
1 8-ounce can crushed pineapple, drained
8 ounces small marshmallows
1 cup chopped walnuts or pecans

½ cup sugar (or desired sweetener equal to
    ½ cup sugar)
2 teaspoons fresh lemon juice
1 12-ounce container Cool Whip
Fresh orange slices or other fruit for garnish

In a large bowl, combine the cranberries, apples, pineapple, marshmallows, walnuts, sugar, and lemon juice and mix well. Fold in Cool Whip. Refrigerate until ready to serve. Garnish the bowl by twisting orange slices or other fruits around the edge.

Mango Chutney Salad

Besides serving mango chutney as a condiment with meat and fish, you can also try mixing it into a salad. It's good with soft-leaved butter lettuce, but if you can't find a good head of that, consider using red-leaf lettuce instead.

Serves 4 to 6

2 mangos, pitted and cubed
1 tablespoon grated nutmeg
1 tablespoon brown sugar
1 tablespoon balsamic vinegar

1 teaspoon cinnamon
Pinch of cayenne pepper
1 head butter lettuce, leaves separated

In a large bowl, combine mangos, nutmeg, sugar, vinegar, cinnamon, and cayenne. Mix well, spoon onto lettuce leaves, and enjoy.

Work It Out

I got into jogging the same way I got involved in healthy eating—by reading about it. I started jogging in Atlanta at the track, and while I was there, I ran into Claude Humphrey, who played football for the Atlanta Falcons. He gave me some pointers about running and encouraged me to keep going.

Not long afterward, I went to San Francisco to do an engagement with Dionne Warwick in San Carlos. While I was there, I met a lady who was an assistant to the hairdresser we were using for the show. I was trying to impress her, so when she said she was a runner, I said that I ran, too. Mind you, I was just starting out.

We said we'd meet at six o'clock the next morning to jog around Lake Merced. We started running, and before we'd gone a half mile, I started breathing hard. I couldn't carry on a conversation anymore, though she, of course, was talking with ease. I'm thinking, *This woman is going to kill me.* Well, shortly after we started, I had to stop. My side was hurting me and I was really winded. I promised myself that I was going to get in shape!

So I did what a lot of people were doing—I bought Jim Fixx's *The Complete Book of Running* and Kenneth Cooper's *The Aerobics Way,* and I just started doing it, one day at a time. Finally I got into good-enough shape that I experienced what they called the runner's high. My heart rate slowed; my breathing got easier and deeper. In fact, at first it scared me because I thought I might be having heart failure! But I just kept going until I got up to ten miles a day. In 1980, I suffered a serious injury while water skiing—a hamstring pull—and I had to stop running for six to eight months. That's when I got back into bodybuilding.

Lu's Shrimp and Tortellini Salad

This recipe got a lot easier to fix when really good tortellini started appearing in the refrigerated section of most supermarkets. (Before that, you had to buy the frozen kind or make it yourself.) Feel free to double this recipe if you are feeding a larger group or want to have leftovers, but *don't* double the spices. Taste it before adding more than is called for in the recipe—usually a little goes a long way. *Serves 4 to 6*

1 pound fresh cheese tortellini
3 tablespoons olive oil
1 pound medium shrimp, shelled, deveined, and cooked
1½ cups coarsely chopped celery
1 8-ounce package frozen green peas
1 cup coarsely chopped red bell pepper
1 cup coarsely chopped yellow bell pepper
1 cup chopped green onions, white and green portions
½ cup grated Parmesan cheese
2 tablespoons minced garlic
2 tablespoons chopped fresh tarragon

2 tablespoons chopped fresh thyme
10 fresh bay leaves, chopped
Lettuce

DRESSING
1½ cups Heinz ketchup
¾ cup Hellmann's mayonnaise
2 tablespoons Gulden's spicy brown mustard
2 tablespoons Heinz pickled cucumber relish
1 package Good Seasons salad dressing mix
Tabasco (optional)
Salt to taste
Freshly ground black pepper to taste

Cook the tortellini according to the directions on package until al dente. Drain well and place in a large bowl. Add the olive oil and toss to coat. Add the shrimp, celery, frozen peas, bell peppers, green onions, Parmesan cheese, garlic, tarragon, thyme, and bay leaves and mix well.

Make the dressing: In a small bowl, combine the ketchup, mayonnaise, mustard, relish, salad dressing mix, Tabasco (if using), salt, and pepper. Mix well and pour over tortellini mixture. Gently toss to coat. Cover and refrigerate at least 2 hours before serving. Serve over a bed of lettuce.

Chef Wendell's Quick Salmon Penne

Pasta dishes can be down-home easy or elegant in their look and flavor, like this one. The ginger works its magic, along with the red onions, to give this luscious cream sauce some extra sizzle.

Serves 4

1 8-ounce package penne pasta
1 tablespoon olive oil
½ red onion, thinly sliced
1 clove garlic, minced
1 teaspoon shredded fresh gingerroot
¼ cup soy milk or heavy cream

1 cup packed cleaned fresh spinach leaves
Pinch of ground white pepper
8 ounces smoked salmon
1 teaspoon chopped fresh parsley
½ cup freshly grated Parmesan cheese

Cook the penne according to the directions on package until al dente. Drain in a colander and keep warm.

In a large skillet, heat the oil over medium-high heat. Add the onion, garlic, and ginger and sauté 3 minutes. Add the soy milk and heat to boiling, stirring. Add the pasta, spinach leaves, and pepper and toss to coat.

Add the salmon to the pasta mixture and pull it apart into thin pieces using 2 forks.

Serve sprinkled with the parsley and Parmesan cheese.

Healing from the Heart

My grandmother first introduced me to alternative medicine when I was a child. Back then, we called it folk medicine, or home remedies. I remember cutting myself one time. Mama went out in the yard and cut some nightshade to make a poultice to put on it, to draw out the poison. In the country, there was always something for whatever ailed you. My grandmother knew all the botanical names of the various herbs and when to apply them. We never thought of it as "alternative medicine"; it was just country healing, but it worked.

Years later, I met my friend Valerie Sheppard in a health food store. Her little boy had cancer, but using a combination of alternative and traditional medicine, he has been in remission more than six years.

Because of her experience and the need she saw to educate people, especially in the black community, about alternative therapies, Valerie founded the Sheppard Foundation, whose stated mission is to "research and inform the public of the most effective, affordable, nontoxic alternative treatments for diseases, both degenerative and terminal." She asked me to come to some health fairs with her, and later she asked me to speak at one. Eventually, I became a spokesperson for the Sheppard Foundation.

What interests me about alternative medicine is its emphasis on prevention, on causes rather than symptoms. Alternative medicine works by helping the body heal itself. I believe that the more you know about your health, your body, and how it works, the better off you are.

CCH Pounder's Creole Seafood Pasta with Artichokes

When she's not playing a doctor on *ER* or commanding the screen in any of dozens of movies, CCH Pounder cooks up dishes like this rich and creamy pasta recipe. The fresher the shellfish, the more extraordinary the flavor, so make a deal with your fish guy to get you the best!

Serves 6

4 tablespoons butter
1 large onion, diced
1 green bell pepper, sliced
1 shallot, minced
1 to 2 cloves garlic, minced
½ minced Scotch Bonnet pepper
Pinch of sea salt
12 colossal shrimp, peeled and deveined
8 mussels, debearded
¼ pound lump crabmeat

½ cup dry white wine
¼ cup heavy cream
1 7-ounce jar marinated artichoke hearts, drained
2 teaspoons chopped fresh parsley
1 8-ounce package angel hair pasta, cooked, drained, and kept warm
1 teaspoon sour cream
1 teaspoon caviar (your choice)

In a large skillet over medium-high heat, melt the butter and quickly add the onion, bell pepper, shallot, garlic, Scotch Bonnet pepper, and salt. Sauté until the onion is softened, about 7 minutes.

Add shrimp, mussels, and crabmeat; cover and cook until mussels open, about 2 minutes.

Add the wine, heat to boiling, and simmer for 30 seconds. Add the heavy cream, heat to boiling, and simmer for 1 minute to thicken slightly.

Remove the pan from the heat. Add the artichokes and parsley, and serve over the pasta. Top with sour cream and caviar.

Anne Archer's Homemade Spaghetti

When I lived out in the country, we made everything from scratch, including all our sauces. But after we moved to the city, we started eating sauce from a jar or can, especially when we had spaghetti. If you've never made your own sauce, or if it's been years since you did more than boil the pasta and open a jar, now is the time—and this is a great recipe. Anne Archer is not only a beautiful and graceful actress (remember her in *Clear and Present Danger* and *Patriot Games*?); she's a terrific cook and a very good friend.   *Serves 8 to 10*

½ cup olive oil

3 large onions, finely chopped

2 celery stalks, finely chopped

1 green bell pepper, finely chopped

1 large carrot, finely chopped

2 cloves garlic, finely chopped

4 pounds ground meat: half chuck, half pork

2 28-ounce cans peeled whole tomatoes,
    cut up

1 10½-ounce can condensed cream of
    mushroom soup

1 10½-ounce can condensed tomato soup

1 8-ounce can sliced mushrooms, drained

1 6-ounce can tomato paste

1 tablespoon salt

1 tablespoon sugar

1 teaspoon dried oregano

1 teaspoon chili powder

1 teaspoon Tabasco sauce

½ teaspoon black pepper

⅛ teaspoon crushed red pepper flakes

1 bay leaf

1 cup grated Parmesan cheese

1½ pounds spaghetti, cooked al dente,
    drained, kept warm

In a Dutch oven, heat the olive oil over medium heat. Add the onions, celery, bell pepper, carrot, and garlic and sauté until onions are slightly browned, about 10 minutes. Add the meat and brown slightly, breaking it up into small pieces with a spoon. Cover and simmer 15 to 20 minutes.

Add the tomatoes and their juice, mushroom soup, tomato soup, mushrooms, tomato paste, salt, sugar, oregano, chili powder, Tabasco, black pepper, pepper flakes, and bay leaf and mix well. Simmer, covered, for at least 3½ hours. Add the Parmesan cheese and cook 30 minutes longer.

Serve over spaghetti.

Baked Rigatoni with Zucchini and Eggplant

I've always loved baseball, and so I wanted to include this recipe that Chef Wendell served to Tommy and Laura Lasorda. This kind of Italian family-style food is good to serve when friends come for a casual dinner. Wendell recommends pairing this recipe with a good bottle of Chianti.

Serves 6 to 8

1 pound rigatoni pasta
1 28-ounce can peeled Italian tomatoes
½ cup vegetable oil
1 large eggplant, cut into ⅓-inch dice
¼ cup extra-virgin olive oil
1 clove garlic, finely chopped
2 large zucchini, halved and sliced

1 medium onion, thinly sliced
¼ cup fresh basil leaves, chopped
1 teaspoon dried oregano
Salt to taste
Freshly ground black pepper to taste
8 ounces mozzarella, shredded
½ cup freshly grated Parmesan cheese

Preheat oven to 350 degrees.

Cook rigatoni in a large pot of salted water, stirring occasionally, until al dente. Drain the pasta, reserving ¼ cup of the cooking water. Return pasta to the pot while preparing the sauce.

Puree the tomatoes with their juices in a blender or food processor and remove the seeds by passing the puree through a fine strainer placed over a bowl.

In large nonstick skillet, heat the vegetable oil over medium-high heat. Add half of the eggplant and cook, stirring occasionally, until golden brown, about 6 minutes. Using a slotted spoon, remove eggplant and place on paper towel to drain excess oil. Repeat procedure with remaining eggplant.

Remove vegetable oil from skillet and add the olive oil. Over medium heat, sauté the garlic until fragrant, about 30 seconds. Add the zucchini and onion and sauté over high heat for 6 minutes.

Add the tomato puree, basil, and oregano. Simmer over medium heat until sauce is reduced, about 15 minutes. Stir in eggplant and season with salt and pepper.

Fold eggplant and zucchini sauce into the rigatoni along with mozzarella and reserved pasta cooking water.

Transfer the pasta to a 13x9-inch baking dish. Sprinkle Parmesan cheese evenly over the top. Bake until heated through, about 15 minutes. Serve the pasta piping hot.

Pumping Up

I was a skinny kid when I was in high school. I couldn't even try out for the football team—when I put the gear on, it hung on me like on a scarecrow. The coach said to me, "Ike, son, go to the locker room. You can do us more proud by singing, representing us that way." My ego was crushed.

But I wasn't ready to give up that easily. I was the kind of kid who, if someone kicked sand in my face at the beach, had to get even. I first started bodybuilding in 1970. I used to go to Gold's Gym in Los Angeles, arriving in a limousine. All the best-known bodybuilders worked out there. (I ran into Arnold Schwarzenegger a few years ago and he told his wife, Maria Shriver, about my coming to the gym in a limo in those days!) I made a lot of friends at Gold's, but I didn't stick with the program. It wasn't until my injury ten years later that I found my way back to the gym.

During my bodybuilding years, I got even more involved in eating for better health. Everybody is seeking the Holy Grail of eternal youth, which doesn't really exist, but I learned a lot about how to retard the aging process. Back in the 1980s, we knew the power of antioxidants, and now the rest of the world has caught up and is using these anti-aging, cancer-fighting formulas.

Ike's Ground Turkey Spaghetti Sauce

Since I often don't have the time to make sauce from scratch when I'm preparing this recipe, I get a little help from Ragú, but you can use any brand of store-bought sauce that you like, or make your own. It's recently gotten a lot easier to find fresh ground turkey breast, which I prefer to use instead of beef when I make spaghetti. For the pasta, I like the Barilla brand.

Serves 4 to 6

2 tablespoons vegetable oil
1 pound lean ground turkey breast
1 tablespoon dried cilantro
¼ teaspoon dried sage
⅛ teaspoon Spike seasoning
⅛ teaspoon garlic powder
⅛ teaspoon salt
⅛ teaspoon dried basil
⅛ teaspoon curry powder
⅛ teaspoon ground Jamaican allspice
⅛ teaspoon Chinese five-spice powder
⅛ teaspoon dried tarragon
⅛ teaspoon dried oregano
⅛ teaspoon ground cumin

1 tablespoon soy sauce
Sea salt to taste
1 cup chopped Vidalia onion
2 cloves garlic, minced
1 red bell pepper, chopped
1 green bell pepper, chopped
1 yellow bell pepper, chopped
1 cup sliced mushrooms
1 8-ounce can crushed tomatoes
1 26-ounce jar Ragú spaghetti sauce
½ cup frozen apple juice concentrate, thawed
About ½ cup spring water
1 pound spaghetti or vermicelli, cooked

In large saucepan, heat vegetable oil over medium heat until hot. Add the turkey and cook, stirring in a scrambling motion to break up the meat, until all moisture has evaporated from the turkey.

Add herbs and spices to the turkey and mix well. When the turkey starts to brown, add the soy sauce and salt. Stir in the onion, garlic, bell peppers, and mushrooms. As the mixture continues to cook, the vegetables will start to steam, and the turkey will absorb the moisture. Let it cook until the vegetables are crisp-tender.

Add the tomatoes and Ragú sauce and mix well. Stir in the apple juice. If the mixture is too thick, add spring water until it has a loose sauce consistency. Simmer the mixture until it is thick.

Serve with cooked spaghetti or vermicelli.

LIGHTS, CAMERA, ACTION!

hen I was growing up in the country, radio was always a big part of my life. It was my first exposure to the world outside my small town. When I was just a little boy, my family used to gather around our battery-run set in the country and listen to the war reports from Europe. We'd also heard the shows and soaps—*Stella Dallas, Backstage Wife, Amos 'n' Andy, Fibber McGee and Molly, The Lone Ranger.* That's when radio was king.

The first black person I heard on the radio—on station WDIA, which still exists—was a man named Nat D. Williams. He's gone now, but he was a hell of a historian. He taught at Booker T. Washington High School, my school's rival in Memphis. His radio show was called *The Sepia Swing Club,* and it was on from four in the afternoon until six in the evening, two full hours. Hearing a black man on the radio back then—wow! His theme was a W. C. Handy song—"Memphis Blues," or "Beale Street Blues." My grandmother liked to listen to a gospel choral group called Wings over Jordan. They sang Negro spirituals like "Up above My Head

I Hear Music in the Air" and "Certainly, Lord." I grew up listening to the radio, and later I enjoyed hearing my records played by DJs around the country. But I don't think I ever imagined I'd end up doing my own show.

I first came to KISS-FM in New York City when I was hired to do promotional spots for them a few years ago. Judy Ellis, the station's general manager, said to me, "I think you can do radio."

I told her, "Well, I think you're crazy." She kept after me until I finally said that I'd think about it. So, I thought about it for a while, and then I just did it.

I love to involve the radio audience in my life beyond the station. I'll call in if I'm out of town, or even if I'm in Europe, so my listeners know I'm thinking about them. Once, I called in from the French Riviera and asked a French lady standing next to me to say something on the air. I said, "*Chérie,* come here," and she said something in French and I added, "Eat your heart out!" When I do a movie, I take my audience on the set with me, and invite the other actors to come on my show. It's a lot of fun and a steady gig that keeps me close to my fans.

Radio led me down another, more surprising, road. Shortly after I started working at KISS-FM, my agent called and told me he had some voiceover work for me. My first thought was, "Yes, a Disney movie!"

"No," he said. "This is an independent operation, two young guys who want you to play this character in an animated TV show. He's a black guy living in South Park, Colorado, an elementary school cook who's supposed to mentor a lot of foul-mouthed kids."

Not me, I thought. *I'm out of here.* But I was talked into a meeting with Matt Stone and Trey Parker, the creators of *South Park.* We hit it off pretty well, but I still thought they were

With James Brown at a KISS-FM radio concert at the Theater at Madison Square Garden, 1998.

crazy. And I had an attitude problem because it wasn't a Disney movie. But they sent me a piece of the script, and I started laughing uncontrollably.

"You guys are crazy," I said. "Who would put you guys up to do this?"

"Nobody put us up to this," they said. "We wrote this with you in mind." Well, I was flattered. And they didn't even know that I'd been a short-order cook when I was still in high school. I've been surprised by how many people have responded to the character of Chef, who's even cut a record of songs from the show (*Chef Aid*).

Now, I've got my own film production company, I'm working on more book projects, and I'm launching a food product line with some of my favorite sauces.

I want to keep trying new things, to expand on what I know and continue to grow as a person. There is so much more that I want to do. My dream is to produce some kind of classical piece that will live past my lifetime—that's really what I want.

The scientists say that the universe is constantly expanding. That notion appeals to me. We all have to continue to expand, always moving in new directions. If we don't, we'll regress and shrink, and our minds and bodies will atrophy. I believe that you can always do something more. You can always learn something new, you can always share something, you can always teach something to someone else. A zest for life and a thirst for knowledge are what keep you young.

Sweet Inspirations: Pies, Cakes, Puddings, and More

Basic Piecrust

This is my grandmother's recipe for the perfect piecrust, and I speak from experience when I tell you that I haven't tasted a better one (and I've eaten a lot of pie!). Use it for any of the pie recipes in this book. You can make it by hand using a pastry blender (as Mama did—remember, we had no electricity out in Covington) or more quickly in a food processor.

Makes 2 crusts

2 cups all-purpose flour
¼ cup sugar
1 teaspoon salt

1½ sticks butter, cut into bits
4 tablespoons shortening, cut into bits
4 to 6 tablespoons ice cold water

First, make sure all the ingredients are cold. In a bowl, combine the flour, sugar, and salt and mix well. Add the butter and shortening.

Using a pastry blender or two knives in a scissors fashion, cut in the butter and shortening until they are coated with the flour mixture and the mixture resembles peas.

Gradually add the water, stirring with a fork until the mixture holds together.

Take the dough out of the bowl and knead 5 or 6 times on a lightly floured surface. During this process, if you notice that the dough is getting too warm and sticky, refrigerate it for about 30 minutes, then finish the kneading.

Wrap the dough in plastic wrap and let it rest in the refrigerator for a couple of hours, or if you are not using it right away, you can freeze it (well wrapped) for a couple of months.

Rushia's Fried Apple or Peach Pies

My grandmother used to make these for my grandfather and me (and for my uncles when they visited). We'd eat them one after another while we listened to our favorite programs on the radio. Whether you start with your own dough or use a Pillsbury ready-made piecrust (which works just as well), try making these the way I do: using a glass or biscuit cutter to make small, individual pies.

Serves 6 to 8

2 tablespoons butter
2 cups small chunks peeled fresh apples or
    peaches
3 tablespoons water
⅓ cup sugar or more, depending on
    sweetness of the fruit
1 teaspoon cinnamon
1 teaspoon lemon juice

1 tablespoon cornstarch mixed with
    1 teaspoon water (optional)

1 Basic Piecrust recipe (see page 171)

Vegetable oil for deep-frying
Confectioner's sugar
Cinnamon for dusting the pies

In a large skillet, melt the butter over medium heat. Add the apples or peaches and toss to coat. Add the water. Stir in the cinnamon, sugar, and lemon juice. Cook until the liquid in the pan becomes syrupy and the fruit is softened. If there is a lot of liquid, stir in the cornstarch mixture and cook until thickened. Cool completely.

Roll out the pastry onto a lightly floured surface. Using a 3-inch round biscuit cutter or overturned glass with a 3-inch diameter, cut the pastry into rounds. Put about 2 tablespoons of the fruit mixture onto each round. Moisten the edge of the pastry with water, then fold the round in half, sealing the edges of the pie by pressing them together with the tines of a fork.

Pour oil to the depth of about 1 inch into a large skillet. Heat the oil to hot but not smoking. Cook the pies, gently turning them once, until they are golden. Drain on paper towels and serve.

If you like, sprinkle the pies with confectioner's sugar or cinnamon.

Canning Fruits with Mama

During the off-season (when there was no cotton to raise or pick), my grandmother canned a lot of fruits and vegetables. The land we lived on had peach trees and apple trees, with way more fruit than we could eat when it was ripe. There were great masses of blackberry bushes along the ditch that ran in front of the house separating the house from the road, and I was often sent out to pick berries for pies and jellies.

There was no more delicious aroma than those apples and peaches stewing on the stove as Mama prepared the mason jars. She'd put the jars in the pressure cooker and then when they were ready, she'd store them on shelves in the smokehouse. When I saw those rows of colorful jars brimming with fruit, I knew we would eat well all winter long.

Blueberry Pie

I have to admit it—I've never tasted blueberries as good as the ones I remember picking and eating when I was a kid! Maybe it's because they were so incredibly fresh, or maybe it's that I knew I'd be enjoying them in a pie only a few hours later. I particularly like using a lattice crust for this pie, because the color of the berries peeking through is so great.   *Serves 6 to 8*

4 to 6 cups fresh blueberries, rinsed and stems removed
½ to 1 cup sugar, depending on the sweetness of the berries
2 tablespoons all-purpose flour
Juice of 1 lemon
1 Basic Piecrust recipe (see page 171)

Preheat oven to 350 degrees.

Combine the berries, sugar, and flour in a large bowl; stir well to coat the berries but be careful not to smash them. Gently stir in the lemon juice.

Divide the piecrust dough in half. On a lightly floured surface, roll out one half to about 1 inch larger in diameter than the pie plate and put it in the pie plate, cutting off any excess dough that hangs over the edge.

Spoon the fruit mixture into the pie shell.

Roll out the remaining half of the piecrust. You can either make a lattice for the top (which I prefer) by slicing the dough into strips and alternating horizontal and vertical over the top of the fruit, or you can keep the top crust in one piece. If you use a solid crust, be sure to vent the top well!

Bake until top is nice and golden and the fruit is bubbling, about 1 hour.

Heather's "So You Want to Be a Millionaire" Millionaire's Pie

Even if you've got a half-empty wallet and nothing much in the bank, this is one dessert that will make you feel like a rich man (or woman)! My daughter Heather, who dances for James Brown, loves to make and eat this pie. (So do I—just another way that we are very close!) Use any fruit you like, and just wait to see what happens. After one bite, your guests will be eating out of your hand.

Serves 8 to 10

½ cup pineapple chunks
½ cup sliced, peeled kiwi
½ cup sliced strawberries
½ cup blueberries
½ cup halved maraschino cherries
½ cup flaked coconut
½ cup sliced bananas
½ cup sliced, peeled peaches
½ cup sliced, peeled apples
½ cup halved green candied cherries

¼ cup sultana raisins
1 14-ounce can Eagle Brand sweetened
   condensed milk
1 teaspoon cinnamon
Pinch of ground ginger
2 8-ounce packages cream cheese, softened
2 8-ounce containers Cool Whip topping
1 cup chopped walnuts
1 graham cracker piecrust, baked

In a large bowl, combine all fruits and mix well. Add the sweetened condensed milk. Sprinkle cinnamon and ginger over the mixture and stir.

Carefully fold in the softened cream cheese and then the Cool Whip until mixed well.

Sprinkle the chopped walnuts on bottom of graham cracker piecrust. Spoon the fruit mixture over the nuts and spread evenly, forming a fluffy pie shape.

Chill and serve.

Zesti-Luv Lemon Meringue Pie

There's something about a lemon meringue pie that always gets my juices flowing, but, I promise you, this home-style recipe bears no resemblance to some of the sticky, tasteless versions you may have eaten over the years. This has real lemon flavor to it, plus the extra "oomph" of orange peel and pineapple. (Don't let the prospect of making the meringue topping get you nervous—just use a clean bowl and separate the egg whites carefully.)

Serves 8 to 10

1 14-ounce can Eagle Brand sweetened condensed milk
6 lemons, juiced
1 orange, juiced
1 egg yolk
1 8-ounce can crushed pineapple, drained
1 7-ounce package moist sweetened coconut flakes

2 tablespoons grated lemon zest
2 tablespoons grated orange zest
1 cup chopped walnuts
1 graham cracker pie shell, baked
1 12-ounce box vanilla wafers
6 egg whites
1 cup sifted confectioner's sugar

Preheat oven to 350 degrees.

In a blender, combine the sweetened condensed milk, lemon juice, orange juice, and egg yolk. Pulse to combine. Pour the mixture into a large bowl and add the pineapple, half of the coconut flakes, and the lemon and orange zest. Mix well.

Sprinkle the walnuts over the bottom of the piecrust and spoon the lemon filling mixture on top. Make a cross of vanilla wafers over the top of the pie. Fill each of the four open parts on the sides of the cross with more wafers, then line the side of the pie with wafers by sinking them into the pie, between the filling and the crust.

Bake until the pie is set and the wafers start to brown. Remove from oven and set aside.

In a large, clean bowl, beat the egg whites with an electric mixer at high speed. When the egg whites are foamy, gradually add the confectioner's sugar. When the sugar is incorporated and the egg whites form stiff peaks, spoon the mixture on top of the pie. Sprinkle the top with the remaining coconut flakes.

Bake the pie until the tips of the meringue begin to brown. Cool the pie and refrigerate until chilled.

Juliette Lewis's Nana's Lemon Meringue Pie

Juliette and I share a weakness for lemon meringue pie, and so I decided to include her family recipe in this book as well as my own version of this luscious dessert. She told me that her grandmother used to make this pie every year for her father's birthday when he was growing up. Juliette added, "And she always made it for me. I love it!" I bet you will, too. *Serves 8 to 10*

10 graham crackers, crumbled
4 tablespoons butter, melted
7 tablespoons sugar
3 egg yolks
1 14-ounce can Eagle Brand sweetened
   condensed milk

4 medium lemons, juiced
3 egg whites
½ teaspoon vanilla extract

Preheat oven to 375 degrees.

In a medium bowl, combine the graham cracker crumbs, melted butter, and 1 tablespoon sugar. Using your fingertips, press the mixture into the bottom and sides of a pie plate.

In a small bowl, whisk together the egg yolks, condensed milk, and lemon juice. Pour into the piecrust.

In a large bowl, using an electric mixer at high speed, beat the egg whites, remaining sugar, and vanilla until stiff peaks form. Cover the lemon filling with the meringue. Bake until the meringue is golden brown, 30 to 45 minutes.

Meeting Elvis

The first time I met Elvis, I was playing at his Christmas party at a place called the Manhattan Club in Memphis. We had two gigs that night. We'd go over to the National Guard Armory and do one set, then run back to Elvis's party and do a set, then back to the armory—back and forth all night long.

Elvis came over to us at one point—this was when they had rails around the bandstand segregating the band (which was black) from the audience (who were white). You couldn't cross that line at intermission; you had to go outside. Elvis shook our hands and said, "Hey, man, you guys sound good." (One thing people did agree on in Memphis was music, which managed to transcend the color line even before the civil rights movement helped end segregation.)

Elvis introduced us to his fiancée, Priscilla. She was very quiet, very beautiful. We're friends now, and we recently reminisced about the night we met. This is one of their daughter Lisa Marie's favorite recipes, about which she declared, "This recipe means to me a good ten pounds gained instantly if you eat it three times a week. When it hits your palate, first you see Jesus, then you meet the digestion devil, and then you get the blues faster than you can say 'Damn, Baby.'"

With Princess Asie Ocansey of Ghana and Lisa Marie Presley
at the Christmas party fund-raiser, 1998.

Lisa Marie Presley's Banana Pudding

A quick note of warning on this recipe—use a fresh box of cream of tartar, especially if the one in your cabinet is a little dusty. Most ingredients tend to lose their pizzazz after three to six months, so make a point of replacing the old stuff.   *Serves 10 to 12*

1 quart milk, chilled
1 8-ounce package vanilla pudding mix
1 12-ounce box vanilla wafers
3 to 4 ripe bananas

MERINGUE
5 egg whites
½ teaspoon cream of tartar
5 tablespoons sugar

Preheat oven to 400 degrees.

Pour the milk into a large bowl and sprinkle pudding mix on top. Beat at low speed for 1 minute, scraping the sides and bottom of the bowl with a rubber spatula. Continue mixing at low speed until smooth, about 4 minutes.

Line the bottom and sides of a 13x9-inch baking dish with the vanilla wafers. Thinly slice bananas and arrange on top. Pour the pudding over the bananas. *Do not stir.*

Make the meringue: In a large, clean bowl, combine the egg whites and cream of tartar. With clean beaters, beat the egg whites at high speed until frothy. Add the sugar, 1 tablespoon at a time, beating continually at high speed until stiff peaks form. Spread the meringue over the pudding. Bake until the meringue is slightly browned, 10 to 12 minutes.

Cool pie. Refrigerate until chilled.

Jenna Elfman's Chocolate Pudding Cake

Jenna Elfman is a talented young star in Hollywood who's got a tremendous zest for life. I've had the pleasure of sitting next to her at dinner parties, and she kindly shared this recipe with me. She told me, "This chocolate chip pudding cake reminds me of how great it was to be a kid, and how my mom used to make it as a treat for us when I was playing with my friends."

Serves 6 to 8

*1 box devil's food cake mix (Mama used
    Duncan Hines)*
*1 3-ounce package chocolate pudding, cooked
    according to package directions*

1 cup chopped walnuts (optional)
1 6-ounce package chocolate chips

Preheat the oven to 350 degrees.

Grease and flour a 13x9-inch baking pan.

In a large bowl, combine the dry cake mix and the prepared pudding. Add the chopped nuts, if using.

Pour the batter into the prepared pan. Sprinkle with chocolate chips, lightly pressing them into the batter.

Bake the cake for 30 minutes. Remove from oven and set aside to cool. Slice and serve.

Janie's Old-Fashioned Pound Cake

I've heard people say they didn't like to order pound cake because it was too "plain" a dessert, but I'd bet they never tasted a true, old-fashioned, made-from-scratch pound cake like this one! This is special-occasion eating, not everyday stuff, and yes, it's very sweet and rich. But why settle for anything less than fantastic when it comes to dessert?   *Serves 10 to 12*

4 sticks butter, softened
3 cups sugar
9 eggs yolks, beaten
4 cups all–purpose flour
½ teaspoon baking powder
¼ teaspoon salt

1 cup milk
9 egg whites, stiffly beaten
1 teaspoon vanilla extract
½ teaspoon lemon extract
1 brown paper bag

Preheat oven to 250 degrees. Grease and flour a large loaf pan and line with paper cut from a brown paper bag.

In a large bowl, beat the butter and sugar at high speed until light and fluffy. Beat in the egg yolks.

In another bowl, combine the flour, baking powder, and salt and sift. Add flour mixture alternately with the milk to the creamed mixture, stirring after each addition.

Fold in the egg whites and add vanilla and lemon extracts. Blend all the ingredients.

Pour the batter into the prepared loaf pan. Bake for 2 hours, until a cake tester inserted in the center comes out clean.

Let the cake cool for 10 minutes in the pan. Remove cake from pan and serve.

Pearlie's Scrumptious Apple Bake
with Whipped Cream Topping

I love walking into Pearlie's kitchen when she's got a pan of this baking in the oven. The aroma of cinnamon, apples, and raisins is downright irresistible! (I've heard that real estate agents recommend to people trying to sell their houses that they put some apples sprinkled with cinnamon and sugar to bake in the oven when anyone comes to look at the place. I bet this recipe would work even better—and you'd have something delicious to eat when they leave!)

Serves 6 to 8

6 to 8 Granny Smith apples, peeled, cored, and sliced
1 lemon, juiced
1 teaspoon grated lemon zest
½ cup raisins
1 cup all-purpose flour
¾ cup sugar
1 teaspoon baking powder
1 teaspoon cinnamon
1 egg yolk
1 stick cold butter, in pieces

WHIPPED TOPPING
2 cups heavy cream, or 2 envelopes dessert topping mix such as Whip It, whipped until stiff, or 1 12-ounce container Cool Whip
2 tablespoons sugar
2 tablespoons Grand Marnier or your favorite liqueur

Preheat oven to 350 degrees. Grease a 12x8-inch Pyrex dish with butter or nonstick cooking spray.

Place the apples in the prepared dish and sprinkle the lemon juice, zest, and raisins on top.

In a food processor fitted with a steel blade, mix the flour, sugar, baking powder, and cinnamon. Add the egg yolk and butter and process until crumbly. Sprinkle mixture over the apples and bake until the top is browned and apples are bubbling, 30 to 40 minutes.

For the whipped topping, whip the heavy cream at high speed until soft peaks form. Beat in the sugar and the Grand Marnier. If using the dessert topping mix or Cool Whip, beat in just the Grand Marnier. Put the topping in a pastry bag and pipe over your scrumptious apple bake while still hot. Have a wonderful evening!

Slammin' Chocolate Pecan Toffee Mousse Pie with "To Die for" Sauce

There are times for eating healthy desserts, and then there are times to *splurge* in a big way. This recipe is one of them, and it's worth every calorie and fat gram! The crust is like a great big praline, and the mousse itself is pure, creamy chocolate heaven. Pour on the toffee sauce, and you'll know with every lick of your being that this is what dessert was meant to be.

Serves 6 to 8

CRUST
1 pound pecan pieces
1 stick unsalted butter
½ cup sugar
¼ cup water

SAUCE
4 sticks unsalted butter
3½ cups sugar
1 quart heavy cream

MOUSSE
28 ounces semisweet chocolate
¼ cup vegetable oil
1 quart heavy cream

Preheat oven to 350 degrees. Butter and flour a 12-inch tart pan.

For the crust: In a food processor fitted with a steel blade, coarsely grind pecans and place in a large bowl. In a small saucepan, melt the butter and add the sugar. Stir and beat until mixture is a thick smooth paste. Remove from heat and add the water, stirring to create a syrup. Pour the mixture over pecans and mix thoroughly. Press the pecan mixture into the prepared pan and bake until golden brown, about 10 minutes. Remove and let cool to room temperature.

For the mousse: In the top of a double boiler set over hot, not boiling water, melt the chocolate and add the vegetable oil. The chocolate mixture should be smooth and have almost liquid consistency. In a large bowl, whip the cream at high speed until soft peaks form. Slowly add the hot chocolate mixture while beating until creamy. Refrigerate the mixture for 2 hours. Spoon mixture into pastry bag and pipe mousse into pecan crust. Refrigerate complete pie.

For the sauce: In a large, deep skillet, melt the butter over medium heat. Add the sugar and cook, stirring, until it is melted. Cook until the mixture is a deep caramel color. At this point, butter and sugar will be separating. Remove from heat and, using a long-handled whisk or wearing an oven mitten, slowly add the heavy cream, stirring constantly. When adding cream, the mixture will bubble up and very hot steam will be released. Strain the sauce into a container and let cool. Keep refrigerated and reheat at serving time.

Ladle toffee sauce over each slice of pie when serving.

Pearlie's Triple Chocolate Trifle

I'm not sure if I first ate the beloved English dessert called trifle while I was living over in London, but those layers of cake and cream and fruit were hard to resist. This is my friend Pearlie's "chocoholic's" version of trifle, and it's even more tempting than the original! If possible, serve this in a big glass bowl so your guests can see each delectable layer. *Serves 8 to 10*

1 box devil's food cake mix
1 cup Kahlúa
3 Heath bars (about 1 to 2 ounces each)
3 1.55-ounce Hershey's chocolate bars

1 3-ounce package Jell-O chocolate pudding mix
1 12-ounce container Cool Whip
Berries, cherries, or other fruit for garnish

Bake cake in a 13x9-inch pan according to package directions. After cake has cooled in the pan for about 15 minutes, cut into small cubes and, leaving them in the pan, pour Kahlúa over cake to soak for a few hours.

Coarsely chop candy bars together in a food processor.

Make the pudding with 1 cup less milk than directed on box.

On the bottom of a trifle bowl, place half of the soaked cake and top with a layer of half of the pudding, then half of the candy pieces and then half of the Cool Whip. Repeat, finishing with Cool Whip on top.

Garnish with berries or other fruits.

Pearlie's Gotta-Have-It-Quick
Peach Cobbler

Instead of starting with sliced fresh peaches, this recipe calls for frozen ones that are then thawed right in the baking crust. (Pearlie told me that doing it this way just makes it taste better when it's done.) To make this even easier to prepare, it also calls for a packaged piecrust. When you gotta have it quick, these shortcuts make sense! *Serves 4 to 6*

FILLING
1 16-ounce package frozen peaches
2 tablespoons all-purpose flour
1 tablespoon cinnamon
½ cup sugar
4 tablespoons unsalted butter
1 tablespoon fresh lemon juice
½ teaspoon ground nutmeg

1 teaspoon vanilla extract
1 teaspoon almond extract

CRUST
1 Betty Crocker prepared piecrust
1 tablespoon unsalted butter, softened
1 tablespoon sugar
1 teaspoon cinnamon

Preheat oven to 400 degrees.

Put frozen peaches in 2-quart baking dish and bake until nearly thawed.

While peaches are thawing in the oven, combine the remaining filling ingredients in a microwave-safe bowl and microwave on high long enough for butter to melt, about 25 seconds. Mix well.

When peaches are thawed, pour the butter mixture over peaches and bake until bubbling, about 20 minutes.

Cover the peach mixture with prepared piecrust. Spread the butter over the crust and sprinkle with sugar and cinnamon. Using a fork, press the edges of piecrust onto the edge of the dish to seal. Make several slits in the top of the pie.

Bake until golden brown, about 15 minutes.

Crazed Carrot Cake

There's just never been a cake as moist as this one, at least in my memory. You can buy carrots already grated if you're short on time, but I like to grate my own using the food processor. This cake is so good it doesn't really need the cream cheese icing that follows. But you know what they say: What's *need* got to do with it?

Serves 8 to 10

2 cups sifted all-purpose flour
2 teaspoon baking powder
1½ teaspoons baking soda
1 teaspoon salt
2 teaspoons cinnamon
1 cup vegetable oil
2 cups sugar
4 eggs
2 cups grated carrots

1½ cups chopped walnuts or pecans
1 8-ounce can crushed pineapple, drained
1 cup raisins
½ cup flaked coconut
1½ teaspoons vanilla extract
Confectioner's sugar
Shaved carrots for garnish
Carrot leaves for garnish

Preheat oven to 350 degrees. Well grease and flour a 13x9-inch baking pan or 2 large loaf pans.

Sift together flour, baking powder, baking soda, salt, and cinnamon. Combine oil and sugar in large mixing bowl, and then beat thoroughly with electric mixer. Add eggs, one at a time, beating well after each. Sift flour mixture into egg mixture and beat thoroughly. Add carrots, nuts, pineapple, raisins, coconut, and vanilla and mix well. Spread batter in the prepared pan.

Bake until the cake tests done in the middle, about 1 hour.

Let cake cool for at least 5 minutes before turning out on cake rack to finish cooling. Dust with sifted confectioner's sugar and garnish with shaved carrots and carrot leaves.

Cream Cheese Icing

This is one of those perfectly simple recipes that every cook should have in his or her repertoire because it's just that: simple and perfect. Just make sure you don't keep tasting it too many times, or you won't have enough left to ice the cake!

2 8-ounce packages cream cheese, softened
¼ cup confectioner's sugar
Fresh lemon juice for taste and consistency

Place cream cheese and confectioner's sugar in a food processor and process until smooth, adding enough lemon juice to get the desired flavor and consistency.

Marinated Aloha Coconut Cake

I loved the coconut cake my aunt used to make for us when we lived in Covington, but I didn't think to ask for her recipe back then. This version comes from my dear friend Pearlie, who knows how to use modern convenience foods and handy ingredients to get that good, old-fashioned taste. Pearlie recommends you wait two days before you slice this cake (letting it rest in the refrigerator). I assure you, it is worth the wait! (The title is something of a misnomer, as nothing is actually "marinated" in the recipe. But it's really moist!)   ***Serves 8 to 10***

CAKE
1 package yellow cake mix
1 3-ounce package vanilla-flavored instant
    pudding and pie filling
1⅓ cups water
4 eggs
¼ cup vegetable oil
2 cups Baker's coconut
½ cup finely chopped walnuts

FILLING/FROSTING
2 cups sugar
2 cups sour cream
1 18-ounce package frozen coconut, thawed
1 8-ounce container Cool Whip

Preheat oven to 350 degrees. Grease and flour 3 9-inch round cake pans.

For the cake: In a large mixing bowl, combine the cake mix, pudding mix, water, eggs, and oil. Using an electric mixer, beat at medium speed until smooth, about 4 minutes. Stir in the coconut and walnuts.

Pour the batter into the prepared pans and bake until a cake tester inserted in centers comes out clean, about 35 minutes.

Cool in pans for 15 minutes before removing them. Place on a wire rack to cool.

For the filling/frosting: In a large bowl, combine the sugar, sour cream, coconut, and Cool Whip and mix well. Frost the cake, including putting filling between the layers and on the sides.

Refrigerate before cutting.

Sweet Brown Sugar Pound Cake

I'm sure you've eaten pound cake before (though maybe never the homemade kind). But this recipe is going to change everything you've ever felt about pound cake, and it's the brown sugar that makes all the difference! It's a little more work than some cakes, because you need to separate the egg whites and yolks, but if you want a rich and light cake, it's definitely worth it.

Serves 8 to 10

4 sticks unsalted butter, softened
1 16-ounce box light brown sugar
½ cup granulated sugar
5 egg yolks, well beaten
3 cups all-purpose flour
1 teaspoon baking powder

1 cup milk
5 egg whites, beaten until stiff
1 cup chopped pecans
2 teaspoons vanilla extract
1 teaspoon fresh lemon juice

Preheat oven to 300 degrees. Grease and flour a 10-inch tube pan.

In a large bowl, with an electric mixer at high speed, cream butter, add sugars, and beat until light and fluffy. Stir in the egg yolks.

In a small bowl, mix flour and baking powder and beat into the butter mixture, a little at a time, alternating with the milk. Fold in the egg whites. Gently stir in the pecans, vanilla, and lemon juice. Bake until a cake tester inserted in the cake comes out clean, about 90 minutes.

Island Punch Bowl Cake

This recipe got its name not because it's flavored with punch (it's not) but because it's designed to be served in a big punch bowl. It's popular with many cooks because it's prepared from ingredients they can find on their pantry shelf. Fancy baking is fine when you've got the time and the inclination, but the rest of the time—layer up this one! (Sometimes I make this cake with a flavored syrup—strawberry, for example—and I blend in fresh cut strawberries instead of cherry pie filling. Or you could use another kind of berry pie filling in a can—whatever you like best.) *Serves 8 to 10*

1 1-pound, 2¼-ounce box yellow cake mix
2 3-ounce packages instant vanilla pudding
    mix
2 1-pound, 5-ounce cans cherry pie filling
2 8-ounce cans pineapple tidbits, drained
2 15¼-ounce cans tropical fruit, drained
1 7-ounce package coconut
1 4-ounce package chopped nuts
1 12-ounce container Cool Whip

Bake the cake according to package directions in 2 8-inch pans and let cool.

Prepare pudding according to package directions.

Place one cake layer in the punch bowl and top, in layers, with half the pudding and the other ingredients in the order given. Repeat, being sure to end with Cool Whip on top.

Refrigerate and serve.

Strawberry Schnapps Shortcake

This is another one of my quick and easy desserts, perfect for serving to unexpected guests as long as you have the ingredients on hand. If you prefer not to use the schnapps, you could substitute a strawberry syrup instead.

Serves 6 to 8

1 16-ounce prepared pound cake
2 cups heavy cream, whipped, or 1 12-ounce
    container Cool Whip
1 pint strawberries, sliced and soaked in
    ½ cup strawberry schnapps

10 strawberries, whole and halved for
    topping and garnish around bottom
    of cake

Cut cake lengthwise into 3 layers.

Spread 2 layers with whipped cream or Cool Whip. Cover with marinated strawberry slices (do not use the liquid).

Put the 3 layers back together, spread sides and top of cake with whipped cream in a swirl design. Decorate the top of the cake and around the base of the cake with whole and halved strawberries.

Slice and serve.

Choco-Meal Chocolate Chip Cookies

If you like chocolate chip cookies (and who doesn't?) but you'd like to make yours a little healthier, do what I do: stir in some oatmeal that has been pulverized in your blender until it's like powder! Your cookies will still have the texture you're used to, but they'll provide more nutrition and lots of great flavor.

Makes about 55 cookies

2 sticks butter, softened
1 cup granulated sugar
1 cup brown sugar
2 eggs
1 teaspoon vanilla extract
2½ cups oatmeal, processed in a food
    processor to a fine powder

2 cups all–purpose flour
1 teaspoon baking powder
1 teaspoon baking soda
½ teaspoon salt
1 12-ounce package chocolate chips
1½ cups chopped walnuts

Preheat oven to 375 degrees.

In a large bowl, beat butter and sugar at high speed until light and fluffy. Beat in the eggs and vanilla. Add the oatmeal, flour, baking powder, baking soda, and salt and mix well. Stir in the chocolate chips and nuts.

Scoop out batter with a small scoop (#40) and place 2 inches apart on a cookie sheet. Bake until golden brown, about 8 minutes.

Southern Tea Cakes

These are sort of a southern sugar cookie, made intensely good by the addition of both vanilla and lemon extract. Served with a tall glass of iced tea, they make a perfect case for old-fashioned southern hospitality. Making guests welcome is something we do really well.   *Yields 6 to 8 dozen 2-inch tea cakes*

1 stick margarine, softened
1 cup sugar
1 egg

1 tablespoon vanilla extract
1 tablespoon lemon extract
2 cups self-rising flour

Preheat oven to 375 degrees.

In a large bowl, combine the margarine and sugar and mix well. Stir in the egg and extracts until blended. Add the flour and stir into a stiff dough.

Roll out the dough onto a floured board. Using cookie cutters, cut out in various shapes. Place on lightly greased or nonstick cookie sheets and bake until golden brown, 6 to 8 minutes.

Sweet Potatoes Versus Yams

Have you ever wondered if there's a difference between what we call sweet potatoes and what are called yams? (I did, too, since I've heard them used interchangeably since I was a kid.) Turns out that yams originated in Africa and are generally available only in the tropics; what we get in our markets are all versions of sweet potatoes, which were found by Columbus on these shores. Slaves brought to this country referred to these orange-fleshed potatoes as *nyamis,* because they resembled the tubers they knew from their homelands. Since then, yams and sweet potatoes have been linked together, although they're from completely different plant families.

Sweet Potato Pie with Walnut Streusel

This pie is a beloved country tradition and served just about everywhere across the South. The streusel topping is what makes this very good pie even more special. Pick out some nice-looking sweet potatoes when you go to the market; if they're too wrinkly and old, you won't get as good a result.

Serves 8 to 10

1 9-inch graham cracker piecrust

FILLING
1½ cups mashed cooked sweet potatoes
⅔ cup granulated sugar
½ cup evaporated skim milk
2 teaspoons vanilla extract
1 teaspoon almond extract
½ teaspoon grated nutmeg
¼ teaspoon mace

¼ teaspoon salt
3 large eggs

STREUSEL
¼ cup all-purpose flour
¼ cup packed dark brown sugar
¾ teaspoon cinnamon
2 tablespoons chilled butter or stick
    margarine, cut into small pieces
¼ cup chopped walnuts

Preheat oven to 350 degrees.

For the filling, in a food processor, combine the sweet potato and the remaining ingredients. Process until smooth and pour into the prepared graham cracker piecrust.

For the streusel, in a medium bowl, combine the flour, brown sugar, and cinnamon and cut in the butter with a pastry blender. Stir in the walnuts. Sprinkle the mixture over the sweet potato filling.

Bake the pie until set, about 45 minutes. Cool on wire rack.

Aunt Akemi's Sweet Potato Pecan Pie with Bourbon Whipped Cream

Even though I don't drink anymore, I've been known to make an exception for the little bit of bourbon in this pie's creamy topping. If you prefer to leave out the bourbon, try a bit of almond or vanilla extract. (Start with half a teaspoonful, and taste before adding more.)

Serves 6 to 8

FLAKY PIECRUST
1⅓ cups all-purpose flour
1 tablespoon sugar
½ teaspoon salt
6 tablespoons chilled unsalted butter,
*   cut into bits*
2 tablespoons chilled solid vegetable
*   shortening, cut into small pieces*
3 tablespoons ice water

SWEET POTATO LAYER
1¾ cups cooked sweet potatoes or yams
¾ cup sugar
2 eggs
½ cup evaporated milk
6 tablespoons butter, melted

2 tablespoons cinnamon
1 tablespoon vanilla extract

PECAN LAYER
2 eggs
⅓ cup sugar
¾ cup light or dark corn syrup
2 tablespoons butter, melted
1 tablespoon vanilla extract
Pinch of salt
1 cup pecan halves and pieces

BOURBON WHIPPED CREAM
3 cups heavy cream, well chilled
½ cup packed light brown sugar
⅓ cup bourbon

Preheat oven to 400 degrees.

For the piecrust: In a medium bowl, combine the flour, sugar, and salt and mix well. Add the butter and shortening and cut in with a pastry blender or two knives used scissors fashion until mixture resembles peas. Sprinkle with the ice water and stir with a fork until the mixture forms a clump. Shape into a disk and roll out onto a lightly floured board to a 10-inch round. Fit into a 9-inch pie plate and trim and flute the edges. Set aside.

For the sweet potato layer: In a medium bowl, combine the sweet potatoes, sugar, eggs, milk, butter, cinnamon, and vanilla and mix well. Pour into the piecrust.

For the pecan layer: In a medium bowl, lightly beat the eggs with the sugar. Add the corn syrup, butter, vanilla, and salt and mix until blended. Stir in the pecans. Pour the mixture over the sweet potato layer and bake pie 10 minutes. Reduce oven temperature to 325 degrees and bake for 1 hour.

For the bourbon whipped cream: In a large bowl, beat cream and sugar at high speed until soft peaks form. Add the bourbon and beat until stiff. Refrigerate until ready to serve on top of pie.

Blackberry Patch Cobbler

My grandmother always made her cobbler in a rectangular pan, using pie dough. She would layer it so you'd get fruit in every mouthful. My sister and I used to pick blackberries by the side of the road. Without fail, though, every time we picked berries my sister would find the snake (or it would find her) in the blackberry patch! *Serves 6 to 8*

1 Basic Piecrust recipe (see page 171)
or 2 ready-made piecrusts
4 cups fresh blackberries

¼ cup all-purpose flour
About ¾ cup sugar
1 stick butter, cut into bits

Preheat oven to 350 degrees. Grease and flour a 10x8-inch baking pan.

Cut the piecrust dough into two parts, one larger than the other. Roll out the larger portion to fit the bottom and sides of the prepared pan.

Place the berries in a large bowl and sprinkle with 2 tablespoons of the flour and about ⅓ cup of the sugar, depending on the sweetness of the berries. Stir to coat the berries.

Begin the layering: Lightly dust the pastry on the bottom of the pan with flour. Spread a layer of fruit over the flour. Top the fruit with a light dusting of the remaining sugar. Dot the top with butter. Repeat this process 2 times.

Roll out the smaller portion of the pastry and cut into strips—longer ones for the length of the pan, shorter ones for the width. Crisscross the dough strips to make a latticework top for the cobbler and sprinkle with sugar.

Bake until the top crust is golden and the fruit is bubbling, about 1 hour.

Serve with your favorite ice cream.

Graham Cracker and Vanilla Wafer Piecrust

Here's a tasty piecrust you can use with all kinds of creamy fillings. A chef friend of mine recommended that I refrigerate this crust before baking it to make it hold together even better.

Makes 1 9-inch pie crust

½ cup graham cracker crumbs
½ cup vanilla wafer crumbs
1 stick butter, melted

1 teaspoon cinnamon
1 teaspoon ground ginger

Preheat oven to 350 degrees.

Pour the crumbs into a deep-dish pie pan. Gradually pour the melted butter into the crumbs, stirring until the butter saturates the crumb mixture.

Press the crumbs into a ⅛-inch-thick crust by hand along the bottom and sides of the pan. Sprinkle the crust with cinnamon and ginger.

Bake until the piecrust starts to brown on the edges, about 10 minutes. Cool before using.

Homemade Chocolate Salty Balls

When I was asked to play the character of Chef on *South Park,* I had no idea where the story might be heading—or that I'd someday be singing about this recipe on *Chef Aid: The South Park Album.* People have asked me how I kept a straight face while singing it, and I can tell you, it wasn't easy. I had to laugh a lot before I could compose myself and really do it. If you're wondering whether Chef is anything like me—well, Chef loves music, women, and sex. And I do, too!

1 cup graham cracker crumbs
¼ cup corn syrup
1 cup milk chocolate chips

⅛ teaspoon salt
3 tablespoons confectioner's sugar

In a medium bowl, combine the graham cracker crumbs and corn syrup and mix well. Using a spoon or a melon baller, shape the mixture into balls.

In the top of a double boiler, slowly melt the chocolate chips. Dip the balls in the chocolate and set the dipped balls on wax paper to set.

On a plate, mix together the salt and sugar. When the chocolate balls are set, roll in the salt and sugar and mixture to lightly coat.

Enjoy.

A Powerful
Thirst

Tennessee Sweetened Iced Tea

This is my preferred way of making iced tea for a crowd. I purchase giant (one-gallon) tea bags at a warehouse store, such as Costco or Sam's Club, then use this recipe to brew up a sweet and delicious pitcherful!

Makes 16 8-ounce glasses

1 giant tea bag
2 cups sugar
1 gallon spring water

Ice cubes
Lemons, sliced

In a large saucepan, boil the tea bag in 1 quart of the water for 1 minute. Take off heat and let stand for 15 minutes.

Add the sugar and stir until dissolved. Pour into a large pitcher or container and add the remaining water. Refrigerate until chilled.

Serve over ice cubes with lemon slices.

Muscatine Wine

Sometimes I'd go with my grandmother to pick Muscatine grapes, which she'd then make into Muscatine wine. She didn't believe in drinking, but she liked to serve the wine when guests came over at Christmastime. She seemed to enjoy the process of making the wine, too, tasting now and again to get it just right. And while I'm not quite sure, I think I remember once or maybe twice that Mama would get a little tipsy. (But I'd never swear to it!)

Country-Flavored Limeade

If your goal is a great-tasting limeade (or lemonade), you can buy pounds of fresh fruit and put your citrus juicer to work squeezing them. It'll fill your house with a wonderful aroma, but it's a lot of work. I'll often purchase a concentrated mixture and add my own special touches—fresh mint leaves, a little bit of freshly grated ginger, cut-up fruits, and even a sprinkle of spices. How sweet you like it is up to you!   *Serves 4 to 6*

Limeade concentrate, or 6 fresh limes
Sugar or other sweetener to taste
Water
2 tablespoons minced fresh gingerroot

Spices and syrups according to taste
4 to 6 mint leaves
12 to 18 pieces fruit (3 pieces per glass), such
   as orange, kiwi, apple, or melon

For each glass, combine limeade with sugar, water, ginger, and spices and mix well. When adding flavor syrups, adjust your sugar accordingly. Put a mint leaf in each glass of flavored limeade. Put at least three pieces of fruit in each glass.

Party Tropical Fruit Punch

These days, lots of people have given up drinking alcohol at parties, but they still want to have a good time—and enjoy a festive beverage. This fruit punch combines some of my favorite juices, and, depending on the fruits you choose as a garnish (star fruit, which is often found in Asian markets, makes a beautiful addition), you can easily set a tropical mood!

Makes about 1 gallon

1 40-ounce bottle white grape juice
2 quarts freshly squeezed orange juice
1 12-ounce can frozen orange juice
1 12-ounce can pineapple juice
12 ounces water

Sugar to taste
Ice cubes
6 lemons, squeezed and sliced
6 oranges, thinly sliced
Several pieces tropical fruit, sliced

Advertisement for the album Juicy Fruit
(Disco Freak), *1976*.

In a large pitcher or container, mix juices, water, and sugar; let set 4 to 6 hours before serving. Pour into punch bowl over ice cubes. Add very thinly sliced lemons, oranges, and tropical fruit.

Hot Apple Cider

Whether you start with a terrific apple cider from your local farmers' market or buy a gallon at the grocery store, don't settle for the taste that comes straight from the jug. Oh, it's already delicious, don't get me wrong—but with a few additions and a little heat in all the right places, you'll be serving a beverage that makes any gathering more special. A note of advice: To avoid hurting your fingers when inserting the cloves, try using an awl or a scissors blade to make small holes in the orange skin.

Makes 32 4-ounce servings

1 gallon apple cider
2 teaspoons whole cloves
2 teaspoons whole allspice
2 teaspoons blades of mace

5 3-inch cinnamon sticks
⅔ cup sugar
3 oranges studded with whole cloves

In a large pot, combine cider, cloves, allspice, mace, cinnamon sticks, and sugar and heat to boiling.

Cover and simmer for 20 minutes.

Strain punch and pour into a heat-safe punch bowl.

Float oranges studded with cloves in bowl.

EATING FOR LIFE

ere's the truth as I've learned it: What you eat is what you are. Even with all the wealth in this country, most of us aren't as healthy as people in some poorer countries. Because they eat only the bare essentials, they suffer from fewer degenerative diseases. (Their problem is fighting infectious diseases, because they don't have access to antibiotics and other means of fighting off infections.) We live in a country with plenty, and we eat plenty. But that's why we have so many health problems.

My diet now mostly consists of fresh, organic vegetables and fruits plus whole grains, healthy foods with the emphasis on *health*. For breakfast, I'll often eat a bowl of brown rice mixed with as many different fresh fruits as I can find. Lunch and dinner are usually a variety of steamed vegetables over grains, and pasta. For me, cooking is still great therapy. It relaxes me.

Another important part of my philosophy of keeping healthy is being aware that mental health is powerfully linked to physical well-being. To put it simply, the mind influences everything about the body. Whatever you focus on, whatever weighs heavily on your mind, you carry with you wherever you go, just as a snail carries his house on his back. The mind is a repository for all that has happened to you over the years. Just as you have to care for your body to keep it healthy, so you need to cleanse and clear out your mind. Otherwise, what you are harboring there becomes "somatic," meaning it can actually manifest itself in physical ways, causing you both mental and physical pain. For optimum health, you've got to learn how to get rid of what weighs you down and holds you back.

That's where the realm of the spiritual can help. Inextricably linked to the mind and the body is the spirit. I have always considered myself a spiritual person. I came here a creature of spirit, and to this day, my spirituality is like a beacon. It's a guide at all times, my navigator. Once you learn to trust the guidance of your spirit, your soul, you will be able to use it to feel better and accomplish more in everything you do. Each of us has abilities that we don't even know we possess. But when we become open to these spiritual gifts, when we start trusting our abilities, they will guide us through the fog and mist, through the roughest parts of life. Too many of us get hung up on the physical realities of our existence, but once we recognize that we are all spiritual beings, we can truly exceed our limits.

With my children and grandchildren. From left, my daughter Nicole;
grandchildren Brittany, Kendrick (on my lap), Raquel,
and Kelvin; and daughter Melanie, 1999.

INDEX

Italics indicate illustrations

My special sauces are now available
for you to enjoy at home.

■

MEMPHIS MAGIC SAUCES

Ike's "I Like It" Barbecue Sauce
Jamaican Jerk Sauce
Tropical Turkey Glaze

■

The proceeds from the sales of these
sauces will benefit music programs at
Manassas High School, Memphis, the
school that helped me become the man
and the musician I wanted to be.

For more information,
visit my website:

www.isaachayes.com